A Special Collection

Illustrated Poems for children

A Special Collection

Illustrated

Poems
for children

Illustrated by **Krystyna Stasiak**

With an introduction by MIRIAM PETERSON, PH.D.
Director of Libraries, Chicago Public Schools

Rand McNally & Company New York / Chicago / San Francisco

Library of Congress Cataloging in Publication Data
Main entry under title:
Illustrated poems for children
  Includes indexes.
  SUMMARY: 159 poems include well-known selections by
Tennyson, Stevenson, Carroll, Housman, Wordsworth,
Dickinson, Frost, Lear, and many other famous poets.
  1. Children's poetry. (1. Poetry—Collections)
I. Stasiak, Krystyna.
PN6110.C4I4 1977 821'.008 77-22105
ISBN 0-528-88584-7
(previously ISBN 0-8331-0019-x)

Printed in Italy

Fourth printing, 1985

Contents

Introduction

by MIRIAM PETERSON, PH.D.
Director of Libraries,
Chicago Public Schools

Poetry, akin to painting and drama, is one of the great art forms. Trying to describe or to explain poetry is difficult — like trying to explain the beauty of a rose or to describe a shooting star. Poetry involves a poet's artful selection of the choicest and most appropriate words to convey a thought or image. It employs rhythm and often rhyme which together with the words intone music and paint pictures.

For children poetry is something to hear, to repeat, and to read aloud, to share, and particularly to enjoy. For adults who would share poetry with children, it is important to be acquainted with poetry of significance and to understand something of its elements and its characteristics.

Both the home and the school share the responsibility and the privilege of helping children to discover and to enjoy good poetry and to build a background of happy experiences with poems of all types and varieties. Poetic verse has many moods and many faces; it encompasses almost all human thought and action and it reaches back to the earliest times of recorded history. Actually it will never cease to exist, for even young children unconsciously yet naturally engage in poetic expression.

Rhythm, rhyme and word pictures are elements common to poetry. These elements, which for very young children predominate in the Mother Goose rhymes, are readily discernible to them as they first listen and then repeat the verses over and over again. Especially if children engage in pantomime they can sense the music and visualize the word pictures.

Poetry should be shared and explored regularly from earliest childhood. Then, as children continue through school, there will be little need to reintroduce or to rediscover poetry through classroom assignments or projects.

Poetry collections are numerous. Some are fat and some are thin; some are general and some are specialized. A collection of poetry reflects the personal interest and taste of its compiler. Each compiler has a particular purpose or focus in mind. Large thick tomes are usually intended for the ready reference shelf; slender volumes are intended as friends and companions to the user. And children as well as adults respond favorably and positively to a volume of poetry when it carries beautiful and colorful illustrations as refreshing and spontaneous as those contained in *Illustrated Poems for Children* .

This book could well be described as a picture book of poetry—a vivid introduction for the young to the wonders of poetry. The elaborate and colorful illustrations reveal the magnificent imagery painted in words by poets. And they not only provide an added beauty to a particular poem but often make the poem immediately understandable to the young child.

There exists a wealth of poetry to delight and enchant young people. In exploring the realms of poetry one encounters poems both old and new created with children in mind as well as those poems enjoyed by adults that children have appropriated and taken to their hearts just as they have the many stories originally directed to adults. The selections for *Illustrated Poems for Children* have been chosen from a gold mine of adult favorites and from poetry written expressly for children. Practically all selections in this uniquely illustrated collection are well-known poems. It is important that children discover and enjoy the best in poetry, for only the best is good enough for tender hearts and minds.

A poem is a very personal and intimate expression of its creator; likewise to the listener and to the reader a poem speaks in a very private way. In a sense, when an individual memorizes a poem and enjoys repeating it he recreates it for his satisfaction, and the poem becomes his own. Poetry should not be spoiled with tedious analysis and explanation. The more a poem is heard the more familiar it becomes, and the listener will perceive greater meaning the more he listens to it and concerns himself with it.

Among the many types of poetry contained in this volume are nonsense verses such as "Eletelephony" to delight the ear of the young child. To laugh, to chuckle, and to be amused are rewarding for both young and old, and nonsense verse to tickle the funny bone is good for the human spirit. Laura Richard's poem should be read aloud again and again for full enjoyment. In a similar yet different vein of nonsense is Ogden Nash's fantastic story-poem entitled "The Tale of Custard the Dragon." In Mary Austin's poem, "The Grizzly Bear," the elements of fancy, absurdity and repetition make for enchanting verse:

> "If you ever, ever, ever meet a grizzly bear,
> You must never, never, never ask him *where*
> He is going."

Poems that include the narrator and the child's point of view can have special appeal such as "The Little Turtle" by Vachel Lindsay:

"He caught the mosquito
   He caught the flea
 He caught the minnow
   But he didn't catch me."

Even for children poetry can be provocative as in the following:

"What is a butterfly? At best
 He's but a caterpillar dressed."

Young people enjoy narration. For them the story is often the thing. The use of tape recorders is becoming popular both in the home and in the school. Encouraging children to record their reading of poetry on tape can help to heighten interest and enjoyment of verse, and narrative poems often lend themselves readily to tape recording. In this collection there are a number of selections that contain plenty of action and vitality such as "Pirate Story" by Robert Louis Stevenson, "The Ghosts of the Buffaloes" by Vachel Lindsay and "Paul Revere's Ride" by Henry Wadsworth Longfellow.

The reader and the listener will encounter whimsy and insight in the poems of Emily Dickinson, nature and wonder in the verses of Christina Rossetti and William Blake, rich imagery and word pictures in the selections from Elinor Wylie and Robert Frost, and the re-creation of a childlike spirit in David McCord's "Everytime I Climb a Tree."

For want of acquaintanceship with the masters, the young are often attracted to the doggerel or to the poets of lesser renown. This collection, however, is highly representative of the great poets beginning with Chaucer and including such poets as Shakespeare, Coleridge, Keats, Shelley and Wordsworth. Other great poets include Blake, Carroll, Frost, De la Mare, Crane, Longfellow, Poe, and Whitman to name a few. And there are selections from recent and contemporary poets such as Langston Hughes, Dorothy Parker, E. E. Cummings, Ogden Nash, David McCord, May Swenson and Karl Shapiro.

The time for poetry should be frequent. It can be a part of the breakfast hour as well as the bedtime routine. In school it can begin and end the day or unite the class after recess or after the noon hour. The home and school bulletin boards can be used for posting best loved poems or for those verses that children have created themselves.

Few poetry books are as charmingly illustrated as this one. The imaginative interpretations, the lovely colorings, the attention to detail, the childlike spirit, and the perceptive understanding characteristic of the artist combine to enchant the reader. They bring additional grace and expression to an inviting collection of significant poems of established reputation. So handsome a volume is a fine addition to a home or to a library.

The Eagle

He clasps the crag with crooked hands;
Close to the sun in lonely lands,
Ringed with the azure world, he stands,

The wrinkled sea beneath him crawls;
He watches from his mountain walls,
And like a thunderbolt he falls.

—ALFRED, LORD TENNYSON

11

Stopping by Woods on a Snowy Evening

Whose woods these are I think I know.
His house is in the village though;
He will not see me stopping here
To watch his woods fill up with snow.

My little horse must think it queer
To stop without a farmhouse near
Between the woods and frozen lake
The darkest evening of the year.

He gives his harness bells a shake
To ask if there is some mistake.
The only other sound's the sweep
Of easy wind and downy flake.

The woods are lovely, dark and deep,
But I have promises to keep,
And miles to go before I sleep,
And miles to go before I sleep.

—ROBERT FROST

The Purist

I give you now Professor Twist,
A conscientious scientist.
Trustees exclaimed, "He never bungles!"
And sent him off to distant jungles.
Camped on a tropic riverside,
One day he missed his loving bride.
She had, the guide informed him later,
Been eaten by an alligator.
Professor Twist could not but smile.
"You mean," he said, "a crocodile."

—OGDEN NASH

I, Too

I, too, sing America.

I am the darker brother.
They send me to eat in the kitchen
When company comes,
But I laugh,
And eat well,
And grow strong.

Tomorrow,
I'll sit at the table
When company comes.
Nobody'll dare
Say to me,
"Eat in the kitchen,"
Then.

Besides,
They'll see how beautiful I am
And be ashamed—

I, too, am America.

—LANGSTON HUGHES

14

This Is Just to Say

I have eaten
the plums
that were in
the icebox

and which
you were probably
saving
for breakfast

Forgive me
they were delicious
so sweet
and so cold

— WILLIAM CARLOS WILLIAMS

Rudolph Is Tired of the City

These buildings are too close to me.
I'd like to PUSH away.
I'd like to live in the country,
And spread my arms all day.

I'd like to spread my breath out, too—
As farmers' sons and daughters do.

I'd tend the cows and chickens.
I'd do the other chores.
Then, all the hours left I'd go
A-SPREADING out-of-doors.

—GWENDOLYN BROOKS

A Tragic Story

There lived a sage in days of yore,
And he a handsome pigtail wore;
But wondered much, and sorrowed more,
    Because it hung behind him.

He mused upon this curious case,
And swore he'd change the pigtail's place,
And have it hanging at his face,
    Not dangling there behind him.

Says he, "The mystery I've found—
I'll turn me round,"—he turned him round;
    But still it hung behind him.

Then round and round, and out and in.
All day the puzzled sage did spin;
In vain—it mattered not a pin—
    The pigtail hung behind him.

And right, and left, and round about,
And up, and down, and in, and out
He turned; but still the pigtail stout
    Hung steadily behind him.

And though his efforts never slack,
And though he twist, and twirl, and tack.
Alas! still faithful to his back,
    The pigtail hangs behind him.

—WILLIAM MAKEPEACE THACKERAY

My Heart Leaps Up

My heart leaps up when I behold
    A rainbow in the sky:
So was it when my life began;
So is it now I am a man;
So be it when I shall grow old,
    Or let me die!
The Child is father of the Man;
And I could wish my days to be
Bound each to each by natural piety.

—WILLIAM WORDSWORTH

The Mountain and the Squirrel

The mountain and the squirrel
Had a quarrel,
And the former called the latter "Little prig":
Bun replied,
"You are doubtless very big;
But all sorts of things and weather
Must be taken in together
To make up a year,
And a sphere.
And I think it no disgrace
To occupy my place.
If I'm not so large as you,
You are not so small as I,
And not half so spry:
I'll not deny you make
A very pretty squirrel track.
Talents differ; all is well and wisely put;
If I cannot carry forests on my back,
Neither can you crack a nut."

— RALPH WALDO EMERSON

When You Are Old

When you are old and gray and full of sleep,
And nodding by the fire, take down this book,
And slowly read, and dream of the soft look
Your eyes had once, and of their shadows deep;

How many loved your moments of glad grace,
And loved your beauty with love false or true;
But one man loved the pilgrim soul in you,
And loved the sorrows of your changing face.

And bending down beside the glowing bars
Murmur, a little sadly, how love fled
And paced upon the mountains overhead
And hid his face amid a crowd of stars.

— W. B. YEATS

The Old Men Admiring Themselves in the Water

I heard the old, old men say,
"Everything alters,
And one by one we drop away."
They had hands like claws, and their knees
Were twisted like the old thorn-trees
By the waters.
I heard the old, old men say,
"All that's beautiful drifts away
Like the waters."

— W. B. YEATS

The Little Turtle

There was a little turtle.
    He lived in a box.
He swam in a puddle.
    He climbed on the rocks.

He snapped at a mosquito.
    He snapped at a flea.
He snapped at a minnow.
    And he snapped at me.

He caught the mosquito.
    He caught the flea.
He caught the minnow.
    But he didn't catch me.

—VACHEL LINDSAY

Little strokes
Fell great oaks.

— ANONYMOUS

Pirate Story

Three of us afloat in the meadow by the swing,
    Three of us aboard in the basket on the lea.
Winds are in the air, they are blowing in the spring;
    And waves are on the meadow like the waves there are at sea.

Where shall we adventure, to-day that we're afloat,
    Wary of the weather and steering by a star?
Shall it be to Africa, a-steering of the boat,
    To Providence, or Babylon, or off to Malabar?

Hi! but here's a squadron a-rowing on the sea—
    Cattle on the meadow a-charging with a roar!
Quick, and we'll escape them, they're as mad as they can be,
    The wicket is the harbor and the garden is the shore.

—ROBERT LOUIS STEVENSON

What Is a Butterfly?

What is a butterfly? At best
He's but a caterpillar dressed.

—ANONYMOUS

Look, Edwin!

Look, Edwin! Do you see that boy
Talking to that other boy?
No, over there by those two men—
Wait, don't look now—now look again.
No, not the one in navy-blue;
That's the one he's talking to.
Sure you see him? Stripèd pants?
Well, *he was born in Paris, France.*

—EDNA ST. VINCENT MILLAY

The Twins

In form and feature, face and limb,
    I grew so like my brother,
That folks got taking me for him,
    And each for one another.
It puzzled all our kith and kin,
    It reached an awful pitch;
For one of us was born a twin,
    Yet not a soul knew which.

One day (to make the matter worse),
    Before our names were fixed,
As we were being washed by nurse
    We got completely mixed;
And thus, you see, by Fate's decree,
    (Or rather nurse's whim),
My brother John got christened *me*,
    And I got christened *him*.

This fatal likeness even dogg'd
    My footsteps when at school,
And I was always getting flogg'd,
    For John turned out a fool.
I put this question hopelessly
    To everyone I knew —
What *would* you do, if you were me,
    To prove that you were *you*?

Our close resemblance turned the tide
    Of my domestic life;
For somehow my intended bride
    Became my brother's wife.
In short, year after year the same
    Absurd mistake went on;
And when I died — the neighbors came
    And buried brother John!

— HENRY S. LEIGH

I Saw a Peacock

I saw a peacock with a fiery tail

I saw a blazing comet drop down hail

I saw a cloud wrapped with ivy round

I saw an oak creep on along the ground

I saw a pismire swallow up a whale

I saw the sea brim full of ale

I saw a Venice glass five fathoms deep

I saw a well full of men's tears that weep

I saw red eyes all of a flaming fire

I saw a house bigger than the moon and higher

I saw the sun at twelve o'clock at night

I saw the man that saw this wondrous sight.

—ANONYMOUS

Humility

Humble we must be, if to heaven we go;
High is the roof there, but the gate is low.

—ROBERT HERRICK

The Sioux

Now what in the world shall we dioux
With the bloody and murderous Sioux
   Who some time ago
   Took an arrow and bow
And raised such a hellabelioux?

—EUGENE FIELD

The Destruction of Sennacherib

The Assyrian came down like the wolf on the fold,
And his cohorts were gleaming in purple and gold;
And the sheen of their spears was like stars on the sea,
When the blue wave rolls nightly on deep Galilee.

Like the leaves of the forest when summer is green,
That host with their banners at sunset were seen:
Like the leaves of the forest when autumn hath blown,
That host on the morrow lay withered and strown.

For the Angel of Death spread his wings on the blast,
And breathed in the face of the foe as he passed;
And the eyes of the sleepers waxed deadly and chill,
And their hearts but once heaved, and forever grew still!

And there lay the steed with his nostril all wide,
But through it there rolled not the breath of his pride:
And the foam of his gasping lay white on the turf,
And cold as the spray of the rock-beating surf.

And there lay the rider distorted and pale,
With the dew on his brow, and the rust on his mail;
And the tents were all silent, the banners alone,
The lances unlifted, the trumpet unblown.

And the widows of Ashur are loud in their wail,
And the idols are broke in the temple of Baal;
And the might of the Gentile, unsmote by the sword,
Hath melted like snow in the glance of the Lord!

—GEORGE GORDON, LORD BYRON

In Just-

In Just-
spring   when the world is mud-
luscious the little
lame balloonman

whistles   far   and wee

and eddieandbill come
running from marbles and
piracies and it's
spring

when the world is puddle-wonderful

the queer
old balloonman whistles
far   and   wee
and bettyandisbel come dancing

from hop-scotch and jump-rope and

it's
spring
and
   the
         goat-footed

balloonMan   whistles
far
and
wee

—E. E. CUMMINGS

Jabberwocky

'Twas brillig, and the slithy toves
   Did gyre and gimble in the wabe;
All mimsy were the borogoves,
    And the mome raths outgrabe.

"Beware the Jabberwock, my son!
   The jaws that bite, the claws that catch!
Beware the Jubjub bird, and shun
    The frumious Bandersnatch!"

Everytime I Climb a Tree

Everytime I climb a tree
Everytime I climb a tree
Everytime I climb a tree
I scrape a leg
Or skin a knee
And everytime I climb a tree
I find some ants
Or dodge a bee
And get the ants
All over me.

And everytime I climb a tree
Where have you been?
They say to me
But don't they know that I am free
Everytime I climb a tree?

I like it best
To spot a nest
That has an egg
Or maybe three.

And then I skin
The other leg
But everytime I climb a tre
I see a lot of things to see
Swallows rooftops and TV
And all the fields and farms
Everytime I climb a tree
Though climbing may be go
It isn't awfully good for pan
But still it's pretty good for
Everytime I climb a tree.

— DAVID MC CORD

He took his vorpal sword in hand:
    Long time the manxome foe he sought—
So rested he by the Tumtum tree,
    And stood awhile in thought.

And as in uffish thought he stood,
    The Jabberwock, with eyes of flame,
Came whiffling through the tulgey wood,
    And burbled as it came!

One, two! One, two! And through and through
    The vorpal blade went snicker-snack!
He left it dead, and with its head
    He went galumphing back.

"And hast thou slain the Jabberwock?
    Come to my arms, my beamish boy!
O frabjous day! Callooh! Callay!"
    He chortled in his joy.

'Twas brillig, and the slithy toves
    Did gyre and gimble in the wabe;
All mimsy were the borogoves,
    And the mome raths outgrabe.

—LEWIS CARROLL

The Wind

I saw you toss the kites on high
And blow the birds about the sky;
And all around I heard you pass,
Like ladies' skirts across the grass—
   O wind, a-blowing all day long,
   O wind, that sings so loud a song!

I saw the different things you did,
But always you yourself you hid.
I felt you push, I heard you call,
I could not see yourself at all—
   O wind, a-blowing all day long,
   O wind, that sings so loud a song!

O you that are so strong and cold,
O blower, are you young or old?
Are you a beast of field and tree,
Or just a stronger child than me?
   O wind, a-blowing all day long,
   O wind, that sings so loud a song!

— ROBERT LOUIS STEVENSON

The Six Badgers

As I was a-hoeing, a-hoeing my lands
Six badgers came up with white wands in their hands.
They made a ring around me and, bowing, they said:
"Hurry home, Farmer George, for the table is spread!
There's pie in the oven, there's beef on the plate:
Hurry home, Farmer George, if you would not be late!"
So homeward I went, but could not understand
Why six fine dog-badgers with white wands in hand
Should seek me out hoeing and bow in a ring,
And all to inform me so common a thing!

—ROBERT GRAVES

The Tale of Custard the Dragon

Belinda lived in a little white house,
With a little black kitten and a little gray mouse,
And a little yellow dog and a little red wagon,
And a realio, trulio, little pet dragon.

Now the name of the little black kitten was Ink,
And the little gray mouse, she called her Blink,
And the little yellow dog was sharp as Mustard,
But the dragon was a coward, and she called him Custard.

Custard the dragon had big sharp teeth,
And spikes on top of him and scales underneath,
Mouth like a fireplace, chimney for a nose,
And realio, trulio daggers on his toes.

Belinda was as brave as a barrel-full of bears,
And Ink and Blink chased lions down the stairs,
Mustard was as brave as a tiger in a rage,
But Custard cried for a nice safe cage.

Belinda tickled him, she tickled him unmerciful,
Ink, Blink and Mustard, they rudely called him Percival,
They all sat laughing in the little red wagon
At the realio, trulio, cowardly dragon.

Belinda giggled till she shook the house,
And Blink said *Weeek!*, which is giggling for a mouse,
Ink and Mustard rudely asked his age,
When Custard cried for a nice safe cage.

Suddenly, suddenly they heard a nasty sound,
And Mustard growled, and they all looked around.
Meowch! cried Ink, and Ooh! cried Belinda,
For there was a pirate, climbing in the winda.

Pistol in his left hand, pistol in his right,
And he held in his teeth a cutlass bright;
His beard was black, one leg was wood.
It was clear that the pirate meant no good.

Belinda paled, and she cried Help! Help!
And Mustard fled with a terrified yelp,
Ink trickled down to the bottom of the household,
And little mouse Blink strategically mouseholed.

But up jumped Custard, snorting like an engine,
Clashed his tail like irons in a dungeon,
With a clatter and a clank and a jangling squirm
He went at the pirate like a robin at a worm.

The pirate gaped at Belinda's dragon,
And gulped some grog from his pocket flagon,
He fired two bullets, but they didn't hit,
And Custard gobbled him, every bit.

Belinda embraced him, Mustard licked him;
No one mourned for his pirate victim.
Ink and Blink in glee did gyrate
Around the dragon that ate the pyrate.

Belinda still lives in her little white house,
With her little black kitten and her little gray mouse,
And her little yellow dog and her little red wagon,
And her realio, trulio, little pet dragon.

Belinda is as brave as a barrel full of bears,
And Ink and Blink chase lions down the stairs,
Mustard is as brave as a tiger in a rage,
But Custard keeps crying for a nice safe cage.

—OGDEN NASH

Tartary

If I were Lord of Tartary,
   Myself and me alone,
My bed should be of ivory,
   Of beaten gold my throne;
And in my court should peacocks flaunt,
And in my forests tigers haunt,
And in my pools great fishes slant
   Their fins athwart the sun.

If I were Lord of Tartary,
   Trumpeters every day
To all my meals should summon me,
   And in my courtyards bray;
And in the evenings lamps should shine
Yellow as honey, red as wine,
While harp and flute and mandoline
   Made music sweet and gay.

If I were Lord of Tartary,
   I'd wear a robe of beads,
White, and gold, and green they'd be—
   And small, and thick as seeds;
And ere should wane the morning star,
I'd don my robe and scimitar,
And zebras seven should draw my car
   Through Tartary's dark glades.

Lord of fruits of Tartary,
   Her rivers silver-pale!
Lord of the hills of Tartary,
   Glen, thicket, wood, and dale!
Her flashing stars, her scented breeze,
Her trembling lakes, like foamless seas,
Her bird-delighting citron-trees
   In every purple vale!

—WALTER DE LA MARE

When Icicles Hang by the Wall

When icicles hang by the wall
    And Dick the shepherd blows his nail
And Tom bears logs into the hall
    And milk comes frozen home in pail,
When blood is nipp'd and ways be foul,
Then nightly sings the staring owl,
                Tu-whit tu-who;
A merry note,
While greasy Joan doth keel the pot.

When all aloud the wind doth blow
    And coughing drowns the parson's saw
And birds sit brooding in the snow
    And Marian's nose looks red and raw,
When roasted crabs hiss in the bowl,
Then nightly sings the staring owl,
                Tu-whit tu-who;
A merry note
While greasy Joan doth keel the pot.

— WILLIAM SHAKESPEARE

Swan Song

Swans sing before they die—'twere no bad thing
Should certain persons die before they sing.

—SAMUEL TAYLOR COLERIDGE

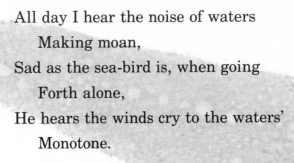

The Noise of Waters

All day I hear the noise of waters
    Making moan,
Sad as the sea-bird is, when going
    Forth alone,
He hears the winds cry to the waters'
    Monotone.

The grey winds, the cold winds are blowing
    Where I go.
I hear the noise of many waters
    Far below.
All day, all night I hear them flowing
    To and fro.

—JAMES JOYCE

Barbara Frietchie

Up from the meadows rich with corn,
Clear in the cool September morn,

The clustered spires of Frederick stand
Green-walled by the hills of Maryland.

Round about them orchards sweep,
Apple and peach tree fruited deep,

Fair as the garden of the Lord
To the eyes of the famished rebel horde,

On that pleasant morn of the early fall
When Lee marched over the mountain wall;

Over the mountains winding down,
Horse and foot, into Frederick town.

Forty flags with their silver stars,
Forty flags with their crimson bars,

Flapped in the morning wind: the sun
Of noon looked down, and saw not one.

Up rose old Barbara Frietchie then,
Bowed with her fourscore years and ten;

Bravest of all in Frederick town,
She took up the flag the men hauled down;

In her attic window the staff she set,
To show that one heart was loyal yet.

Up the street came the rebel tread,
Stonewall Jackson riding ahead.

Under his slouched hat left and right
He glanced; the old flag met his sight.

"Halt!"—the dust-brown ranks stood fast,
"Fire!"—out blazed the rifle-blast.

It shivered the window, pane and sash;
It rent the banner with seam and gash.

Quick as it fell, from the broken staff
Dame Barbara snatched the silken scarf.

She leaned far out on the window-sill,
And shook it forth with a royal will.

"Shoot, if you must, this old gray head,
But spare your country's flag," she said.

A shade of sadness, a blush of shame,
Over the face of the leader came;

The nobler nature within him stirred
To life at that woman's deed and word;

"Who touches a hair of yon gray head
Dies like a dog! March on!" he said.

All day long through Frederick street
Sounded the tread of marching feet:

All day long that free flag tossed
Over the heads of the rebel host.

Ever its torn folds rose and fell
On the loyal winds that loved it well;

And through the hill-gaps sunset light
Shone over it with a warm good-night.

Barbara Frietchie's work is o'er,
And the Rebel rides on his raids no more.

Honor to her! and let a tear
Fall, for her sake, on Stonewall's bier.

Over Barbara Frietchie's grave,
Flag of Freedom and Union, wave!

Peace and order and beauty draw
Round thy symbol of light and law;

And ever the stars above look down
On thy stars below in Frederick town!

—JOHN GREENLEAF WHITTIER

A Bird Came Down the Walk

A bird came down the walk;
He did not know I saw;
He bit an angle-worm in halves
And ate the fellow, raw.

And then he drank a dew
From a convenient grass,
And then hopped sidewise to the wall
To let a beetle pass.

He glanced with rapid eyes
That hurried all abroad,—
They looked like frightened beads, I thought
He stirred his velvet head

Like one in danger; cautious,
I offered him a crumb,
And he unrolled his feathers
And rowed him softer home

Than oars divide the ocean,
Too silver for a seam,
Or butterflies, off banks of noon,
Leap, plashless, as they swim.

—EMILY DICKINSON

The Village Blacksmith

Under a spreading chestnut tree
    The village smithy stands;
The smith, a mighty man is he,
    With large and sinewy hands;
And the muscles of his brawny arms
    Are strong as iron bands.

His hair is crisp, and black, and long,
    His face is like the tan;
His brow is wet with honest sweat,
    He earns whate'er he can,
And looks the whole world in the face,
    For he owes not any man.

Week in, week out, from morn till night,
    You can hear his bellows blow;
You can hear him swing his heavy sledge,
    With measured beat and slow,
Like a sexton ringing the village bell,
    When the evening sun is low.

And children coming home from school
    Look in at the open door;
They love to see the flaming forge,
    And hear the bellows roar,
And catch the burning sparks that fly
    Like chaff from a threshing floor.

He goes on Sunday to the church,
    And sits among his boys;
He hears the parson pray and preach,
    He hears his daughter's voice,
Singing in the village choir,
    And it makes his heart rejoice.

It sounds to him like her mother's voice,
    Singing in Paradise!
He needs must think of her once more,
    How in the grave she lies;
And with his hard, rough hand he wipes
    A tear out of his eyes.

Toiling — rejoicing — sorrowing,
    Onward through life he goes;
Each morning sees some task begin,
    Each evening sees its close;
Something attempted, something done,
    Has earned a night's repose.

Thanks, thanks to thee, my worthy friend,
    For the lesson thou hast taught!
Thus at the flaming forge of life
    Our fortunes must be wrought;
Thus on its sounding anvil shaped
    Each burning deed and thought!

— HENRY WADSWORTH LONGFELLOW

From the Canterbury Tales

A MILLER

The Miller, stout and sturdy as the stones,
Delighted in his muscles and big bones;
They served him well; at fair and tournament
He took the wrestling prize where'er he went.
He was short-shouldered, broad, knotty and tough;
He'd tear a door down easily enough
Or break it, charging thickly with his head.
His beard, like any sow or fox, was red,
And broadly built, as though it were a spade.
Upon the tiptop of his nose he had
A wart, and thereon stood a tuft of hairs,
Bright as the bristles of a red sow's ears.
His nostrils matched the miller, black and wide.
He bore a sword and buckler by his side.
His mouth was broad as a great furnace door.
He loved to tell a joke, and boast, and roar
About his many sins and deviltries;
He stole, and multiplied his thefts by threes.
And yet he had a thumb of gold, 'tis true.
He wore a white coat and a hood of blue,
And he could blow the bagpipe up and down—
And with a tune he brought us out of town.

—GEOFFREY CHAUCER
Modern Version by Louis Untermeyer

Spring

Sound the flute!
Now it's mute.
Birds delight
Day and Night;
Nightingale
In the dale,
Lark in Sky,
Merrily,
Merrily, merrily, to welcome in the Year.

Little Boy,
Full of joy;
Little Girl,
Sweet and small;
Cock does crow,

So do you;
Merry voice,
Infant noise,
Merrily, merrily, to welcome in the Year.

Little Lamb
Here I am;
Come and lick
My white neck;
Let me pull
Your soft Wool;
Let me kiss
Your soft face;
Merrily, merrily, we welcome in the Year.

—WILLIAM BLAKE

The Tiger

Tiger! Tiger! burning bright
In the forests of the night,
What immortal hand or eye
Could frame thy fearful symmetry?

In what distant deeps or skies
Burnt the fire of thine eyes?
On what wings dare he aspire?
What the hand dare seize the fire?

And what shoulder, and what art,
Could twist the sinews of thy heart?
And when thy heart began to beat,
What dread hand? and what dread feet?

What the hammer? what the chain?
In what furnace was thy brain?
What the anvil? what dread grasp
Dare its deadly terrors clasp?

When the stars threw down their spears
And watered heaven with their tears,
Did he smile his work to see?
Did he who made the Lamb make thee?

Tiger! Tiger! burning bright
In the forests of the night,
What immortal hand or eye
Dare frame thy fearful symmetry?

— WILLIAM BLAKE

The Raggedy Man

O The Raggedy Man! He works fer Pa;
An' he's the goodest man ever you saw!
He comes to our house every day,
An' waters the horses, an' feeds 'em hay;
An' he opens the shed—an' we all ist laugh
When he drives out our little old wobble-ly calf;
An' nen—ef our hired girl says he can—
He milks the cow fer 'Lizabuth Ann.—
  Ain't he a' awful good Raggedy Man?
    Raggedy! Raggedy! Raggedy Man!

W'y, The Raggedy Man—he's ist so good
He splits the kindlin' an' chops the wood;
An' nen he spades in our garden, too,
An' does most things 'at *boys* can't do!—
He clumbed clean up in our big tree
An' shooked a' apple down fer me—
An' nother'n', too, fer 'Lizabuth Ann—
An' nother'n', too, fer The Raggedy Man.—
  Ain't he a' awful kind Raggedy Man?
    Raggedy! Raggedy! Raggedy Man!

An' The Raggedy Man, he knows most rhymes
An' tells 'em, ef I be good, sometimes:
Knows 'bout Giunts, an' Griffuns, an' Elves,
An' the Squidgicum-Squees 'at swallers therselves!
An' wite by the pump in our pasture-lot,
He showed me the hole 'at the Wunks is got,
'At lives 'way deep in the ground, an' can
Turn into me, er 'Lizabuth Ann,
Er Ma er Pa er The Raggedy Man!
    Ain't he a funny old Raggedy Man?
      Raggedy! Raggedy! Raggedy Man!

The Raggedy Man—one time when he
Wuz makin' a little bow-'n'-orry fer me,
Says "When *you're* big like your Pa is,
Air *you* go' to keep a fine store like his—
An' be a rich merchunt—an' wear fine clothes?—
Er what air you go' to be, goodness knows!"
An' nen he laughed at 'Lizabuth Ann,
An' I says "'M go' to be a Raggedy Man!—
    I'm ist go' to be a nice Raggedy Man!
      Raggedy! Raggedy! Raggedy Man!"

—JAMES WHITCOMB RILEY

Spanish Johnny

The old West, the old time,
　　The old wind singing through
The red, red grass a thousand miles—
　　And, Spanish Johnny, you!
He'd sit beside the water ditch
　　When all his herd was in,
And never mind a child, but sing
　　To his mandolin.

The big stars, the blue night,
　　The moon-enchanted lane;
The olive man who never spoke,
　　But sang the songs of Spain.
His speech with men was wicked talk—
　　To hear it was a sin;
But those were golden things he said
　　To his mandolin.

The gold songs, the gold stars,
　　The word so golden then;
And the hand so tender to a child—
　　Had killed so many men.
He died a hard death long ago
　　Before the Road came in—
The night before he swung, he sang
　　To his mandolin.

—WILLA CATHER

Be Like the Bird

Be like the bird, who
Halting in his flight
On limb too slight
Feels it give way beneath him,
Yet sings
Knowing he hath wings.

—VICTOR HUGO

A Shropshire Lad

The street sounds to the soldiers' tread,
  And out we troop to see:
A single redcoat turns his head,
  He turns and looks at me.

My man, from sky to sky's so far,
  We never crossed before;
Such leagues apart the world's ends are,
  We're like to meet no more;

What thoughts at heart have you and I
  We cannot stop to tell;
But dead or living, drunk or dry,
  Soldier, I wish you well.

— A. E. HOUSMAN

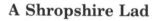

Inventory

Four be the things I am wiser to know:
Idleness, sorrow, a friend, and a foe.

Four be the things I'd been better without:
Love, curiosity, freckles, and doubt.

Three be the things I shall never attain:
Envy, content, and sufficient champagne.

Three be the things I shall have till I die:
Laughter and hope and a sock in the eye.

—DOROTHY PARKER

I May, I Might, I Must

If you will tell me why the fen
appears impassable, I then
will tell you why I think that I
can get across it if I try.

—MARIANNE MOORE

59

The Butterfly's Ball

Come take up your hats, and away let us haste,
To the Butterfly's Ball, and the Grasshopper's Feast.
The trumpeter Gadfly has summoned the crew,
And the revels are now only waiting for you.

On the smooth-shaven grass by the side of a wood,
Beneath a broad oak which for ages has stood,
See the children of earth and the tenants of air,
For an evening's amusement together repair.

And there came the Beetle, so blind and so black,
Who carried the Emmet, his friend, on his back.
And there came the Gnat, and the Dragonfly too,
And all their relations, green, orange, and blue.

And there came the Moth, with her plumage of down,
And the Hornet, with jacket of yellow and brown;
Who with him the Wasp, his companion, did bring,
But they promised that evening, to lay by their sting.

Then the sly little Dormouse crept out of his hole,
And led to the feast his blind cousin the Mole.
And the Snail, with his horns peeping out of his shell,
Came, fatigued with the distance, the length of an ell.

A mushroom their table, and on it was laid
A water-dock leaf, which a tablecloth made.
The viands were various, to each of their taste,
And the Bee brought the honey to sweeten the feast.

With steps most majestic the Snail did advance,
And he promised the gazers a minuet to dance;
But they all laughed so loud that he drew in his head,
And went in his own little chamber to bed.

Then, as evening gave way to the shadows of night,
Their watchman, the Glow-worm, came out with his light.
So home let us hasten, while yet we can see;
For no watchman is waiting for you and for me.

—WILLIAM ROSCOE

The Cloud

I bring fresh showers for the thirsting flowers,
    From the seas and the streams;
I bear light shade for the leaves when laid
    In their noonday dreams.
From my wings are shaken the dews that waken
    The sweet buds every one,
When rocked to rest on their mother's breast,
    As she dances about the sun.
I wield the flail of the lashing hail,
    And whiten the green plains under;
And then again I dissolve it in rain,
    And laugh as I pass in thunder.

—PERCY BYSSHE SHELLEY

The Chickadee

Piped a tiny voice hard by,
Gay and polite, a cheerful cry,
"Chic-chicadee-dee!" Saucy note
Out of a sound heart and a merry throat,
As if it said, "Good day, good sir.
Fine afternoon, old passenger!
Happy to meet you in these places
When January brings new faces!"

— RALPH WALDO EMERSON

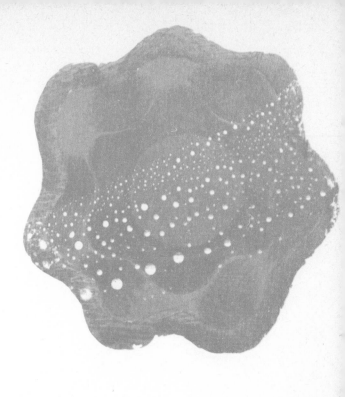

Boy with His Hair Cut Short

Sunday shuts down on this twentieth-century evening.
The L passes. Twilight and bulb define
the brown room, the overstuffed plum sofa,
the boy, and the girl's thin hands above his head.
A neighbor's radio sings stocks, news, serenade.

He sits at the table, head down, the young clear neck exposed,
watching the drugstore sign from the tail of his eye;
tattoo, neon, until the eye blears, while his
solicitous tall sister, simple in blue, bending
behind him, cuts his hair with her cheap shears.

The arrow's electric red always reaches its mark,
successful neon! He coughs, impressed by that precision.
His child's forehead, forever protected by his cap,
is bleached against the lamplight as he turns head
and steadies to let the snippets drop.

Erasing the failure of weeks with level fingers,
she sleeks the fine hair, combing: "You'll look fine tomorrow!
You'll surely find something; they can't keep turning you down;
the finest gentleman's not so trim as you!" Smiling, he raises
the adolescent forehead wrinkling ironic now.

He sees his decent suit laid out, new-pressed,
his carfare on the shelf. He lets his head fall, meeting
her earnest hopeless look, seeing the sharp blades splitting,
the darkened room, the impersonal sign, her motion,
the blue vein, bright on her temple, pitifully beating.

—MURIEL RUKEYSER

Central Park at Dusk

Buildings above the leafless trees
    Loom high as castles in a dream,
While one by one the lamps come out
    To thread the twilight with a gleam.

There is no sign of leaf or bud,
    A hush is over everything—
Silent as women wait for love,
    The world is waiting for the spring.

—SARA TEASDALE

Manhole Covers

The beauty of manhole covers—what of that?
Like medals struck by a great savage khan,
Like Mayan calendar stones, unliftable, indecipherable,
Not like old electrum, chased and scored,
Mottoed and sculptured to a turn,
But notched and whelked and pocked and smashed
With the great company names:
Gentle Bethlehem, smiling United States.
This rustproof artifact of my street,
Long after roads are melted away, will lie
Sidewise in the graves of the iron-old world,
Bitten at the edges,
Strong with its cryptic American,
Its dated beauty.

—KARL SHAPIRO

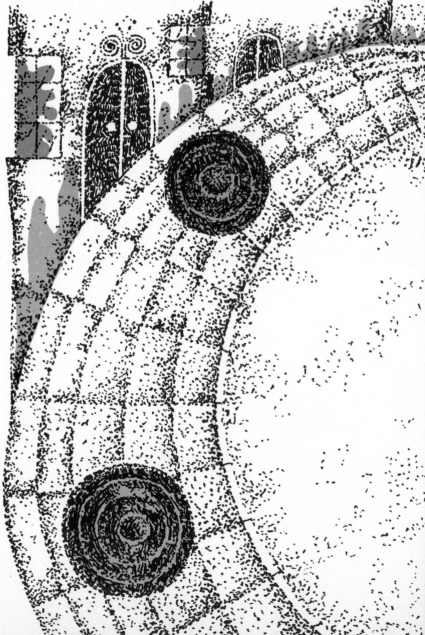

The Snow

It sifts from leaden sieves,
It powders all the wood,
It fills with alabaster wool
The wrinkles of the road.

It makes an even face
Of mountain and of plain,—
Unbroken forehead from the east
Unto the east again.

It reaches to the fence,
It wraps it, rail by rail,
Till it is lost in fleeces;
It flings a crystal veil

On stump and stack and stem,—
The summer's empty room,
Acres of seams where harvests were
Recordless, but for them.

It ruffles wrists of posts,
As ankles of a queen,—
Then stills its artisans like ghosts,
Denying they have been.

—EMILY DICKINSON

The Moon's the North Wind's Cooky

The Moon's the North Wind's cooky.
He bites it, day by day,
Until there's but a rim of scraps
That crumble all away.

The South Wind is a baker.
He kneads clouds in his den,
And bakes a crisp new moon *that . . . greedy*
North . . . Wind . . . eats . . . again!

— VACHEL LINDSAY

I'm Nobody! Who Are You?

I'm nobody! Who are you?
Are you nobody, too?
Then there's a pair of us — don't tell!
They'd banish us, you know.

How dreary to be somebody!
How public, like a frog
To tell your name the livelong day
To an admiring bog!

— EMILY DICKINSON

Snow

Snow descends sugar softly
And whirling white begins to spin.
The highlands drift unevenly
Like brocaded silk and satin.

Great mounds of frost flow gently
Covering hill and dale as well;
For flakes of quiet beauty
Care little where they dwell.

Snow crystals fall so easily
Always in fantastic shapes,
Designs that dance so gracefully
In delicate cloud-escapes.

Icy castles everywhere
Hear all the children laughing,
Warm music fills the frozen air
With the sweetness of their singing.

—STEPHEN TITRA

Annabel Lee

It was many and many a year ago,
    In a kingdom by the sea,
That a maiden there lived whom you may know
    By the name of Annabel Lee;
And this maiden she lived with no other thought
    Than to love and be loved by me.

I was a child and *she* was a child,
    In this kingdom by the sea,
But we loved with a love that was more than love,
    I and my Annabel Lee;
With a love that the winged seraphs of heaven
    Coveted her and me.

And this was the reason that, long ago,
    In this kingdom by the sea,
A wind blew out of a cloud, chilling
    My beautiful Annabel Lee;
So that her highborn kinsmen came
    And bore her away from me,
To shut her up in a sepulchre
    In this kingdom by the sea.

The angels, not half so happy in heaven,
　　Went envying her and me;
Yes! that was the reason (as all men know,
　　In this kingdom by the sea)
That the wind came out of the cloud by night,
　　Chilling and killing my Annabel Lee.

But our love it was stronger by far than the love
　　Of those who were older than we,
　　Of many far wiser than we;
And neither the angels in heaven above,
　　Nor the demons down under the sea,
Can ever dissever my soul from the soul
　　Of the beautiful Annabel Lee:

For the moon never beams, without bringing me dreams
　　Of the beautiful Annabel Lee;
And the stars never rise, but I see the bright eyes
　　Of the beautiful Annabel Lee;
And so, all the night-tide, I lie down by the side
Of my darling—my darling—my life and my bride,
　　In her sepulchre there by the sea,
　　In her tomb by the sounding sea.

—EDGAR ALLAN POE

The Peacock Has a Score of Eyes

The peacock has a score of eyes,
　　With which he cannot see;
The cod-fish has a silent sound,
　　However that may be;

No dandelions tell the time,
　　Although they turn to clocks;
Cat's-cradle does not hold the cat,
　　Nor foxglove fit the fox.

— CHRISTINA ROSSETTI

The Roman Road

The Roman Road runs straight and bare
As the pale parting-line in hair
Across the heath. And thoughtful men
Contrast its days of Now and Then,
And delve, and measure, and compare;

Visioning on the vacant air
Helmed legionnaires, who proudly rear
The Eagle, as they pace again
                    The Roman Road.

But no tall brass-helmed legionnaire
Haunts it for me. Uprises there
A mother's form upon my ken,
Guiding my infant steps, as when
We walked that ancient thoroughfare,
                    The Roman Road.

—THOMAS HARDY

Zebra

The eagle's shadow runs across the plain,
Towards the distant, nameless, air-blue mountains.
But the shadows of the round young Zebra
Sit close between their delicate hoofs all day,
    where they stand immovable,
And wait for the evening, wait to stretch out, blue,
Upon a plain, painted brick-red by the sunset,
And to wander to the water-hole.

— ISAK DINESEN

Little Billee

There were three sailors of Bristol city
Who took a boat and went to sea.
But first with beef and captain's biscuits
And pickled pork they loaded she.

There was gorging Jack and guzzling Jimmy,
And the youngest he was little Billee.
Now when they got as far as the Equator
They'd nothing left but one split pea.

Says gorging Jack to guzzling Jimmy,
"I am extremely hungaree."
To gorging Jack says guzzling Jimmy,
"We've nothing left, us must eat we."

Says gorging Jack to guzzling Jimmy,
"With one another we shouldn't agree!
There's little Bill, he's young and tender,
We're old and tough, so let's eat he."

"Oh! Billy, we're going to kill and eat you.
So undo the button of your chemie."
When Bill received this information
He used his pocket handkerchie.

"First let me say my catechism,
Which my poor mammy taught to me."
"Make haste, make haste," says guzzling Jimmy,
While Jack pulled out his snickersnee.

So Billy went up to the main-top gallant mast,
And down he fell on his bended knee.
He scarce had come to the twelfth commandment
When up he jumps, "There's land I see:

"Jerusalem and Madagascar,
And North and South Amerikee:
There's the British flag a-riding at anchor,
With Admiral Napier, K.C.B."

So when they got aboard of the Admiral's,
He hanged fat Jack and flogged Jimmee;
But as for little Bill he made him
The Captain of a Seventy-three.

— WILLIAM MAKEPEACE THACKERAY

When Fishes Set Umbrellas Up

When fishes set umbrellas up
  If the rain-drops run,
Lizards will want their parasols
  To shade them from the sun.

—CHRISTINA ROSSETTI

The Kitten at Play

See the kitten on the wall,
Sporting with the leaves that fall,
Withered leaves, one, two and three
Falling from the elder tree,
Through the calm and frosty air
Of the morning bright and fair.

See the kitten, how she starts,
Crouches, stretches, paws and darts;
With a tiger-leap half way
Now she meets her coming prey.
Lets it go as fast and then
Has it in her power again.

Now she works with three and four,
Like an Indian conjurer;
Quick as he in feats of art,
Gracefully she plays her part;
Yet were gazing thousands there;
What would little Tabby care?

— WILLIAM WORDSWORTH

The Raven

Once upon a midnight dreary, while I pondered, weak and weary,
Over many a quaint and curious volume of forgotten lore—
While I nodded, nearly napping, suddenly there came a tapping,
As of some one gently rapping, rapping at my chamber door.
" 'Tis some visitor," I muttered, "tapping at my chamber door—
      Only this and nothing more."

Ah, distinctly I remember it was in the bleak December;
And each separate dying ember wrought its ghost upon the floor.
Eagerly I wished the morrow;—vainly I had sought to borrow
From my books surcease of sorrow—sorrow for the lost Lenore—
For the rare and radiant maiden whom the angels name Lenore—
      Nameless *here* for evermore.

And the silken, sad, uncertain rustling of each purple curtain
Thrilled me—filled me with fantastic terrors never felt before;
So that now, to still the beating of my heart, I stood repeating,
" 'Tis some visitor entreating entrance at my chamber door;—
      This it is and nothing more."

Presently my soul grew stronger; hesitating then no longer,
"Sir," said I, "or Madam, truly your forgiveness I implore;
But the fact is I was napping, and so gently you came rapping,
And so faintly you came tapping, tapping at my chamber door,
That I scarce was sure I heard you"—here I opened wide the door;—
      Darkness there and nothing more.

Deep into that darkness peering, long I stood there wondering,
    fearing,
Doubting, dreaming dreams no mortal ever dared to dream before;
But the silence was unbroken, and the stillness gave no token,
And the only word there spoken was the whispered word, "Lenore?"
This I whispered, and an echo murmured back the word "Lenore!"
      Merely this and nothing more.

Back into the chamber turning, all my soul within me burning,
Soon again I heard a tapping somewhat louder than before.
"Surely," said I, "surely that is something at my window lattice;
Let me see, then, what thereat is, and this mystery explore—
Let my heart be still a moment and this mystery explore;—
      'Tis the wind and nothing more!"

Open here I flung the shutter, when, with many a flirt and flutter,
In there stepped a stately Raven of the saintly days of yore;
Not the least obeisance made he; not a minute stopped or stayed he;
But, with mien of lord or lady, perched above my chamber door—
Perched upon a bust of Pallas just above my chamber door—
                    Perched, and sat, and nothing more.

Then this ebony bird beguiling my sad fancy into smiling,
By the grave and stern decorum of the countenance it wore,
"Though thy crest be shorn and shaven, thou," I said, "art sure no
    craven,
Ghastly grim and ancient Raven wandering from the Nightly shore—
Tell me what thy lordly name is on the Night's Plutonian shore!"
                    Quoth the Raven, "Nevermore."

Much I marvelled this ungainly fowl to hear discourse so plainly,
Though its answer little meaning—little relevancy bore;
For we cannot help agreeing that no living human being
Ever yet was blessed with seeing bird above his chamber door—
Bird or beast upon the sculptured bust above his chamber door,
                    With such name as "Nevermore."

But the Raven, sitting lonely on the placid bust, spoke only
That one word, as if his soul in that one word he did outpour.
Nothing farther then he uttered—not a feather then he fluttered—
Till I scarcely more than muttered, "Other friends have flown before—
On the morrow *he* will leave me, as my Hopes have flown before."
                    Then the bird said, "Nevermore."

Startled at the stillness broken by reply so aptly spoken,
"Doubtless," said I, "what it utters is its only stock and store
Caught from some unhappy master whom unmerciful Disaster
Followed fast and followed faster till his songs one burden bore—
Till the dirges of his Hope that melancholy burden bore
                    Of 'Never—nevermore.'"

But the Raven still beguiling all my fancy into smiling,
Straight I wheeled a cushioned seat in front of bird, and bust and door;
Then, upon the velvet sinking, I betook myself to linking
Fancy unto fancy, thinking what this ominous bird of yore—
What this grim, ungainly, ghastly, gaunt, and ominous bird of yore
                    Meant in croaking "Nevermore."

This I sat engaged in guessing, but no syllable expressing
To the fowl whose fiery eyes now burned into my bosom's core;
This and more I sat divining, with my head at ease reclining
On the cushion's velvet lining that the lamp-light gloated o'er,
But whose velvet-violet lining with the lamp-light gloating o'er,
      She shall press, ah, nevermore!

Then, methought, the air grew denser, perfumed from an unseen censer
Swung by Seraphim whose foot-falls tinkled on the tufted floor.
"Wretch," I cried, "thy God hath lent thee—by these angels he
    hath sent thee
Respite—respite and nepenthe from thy memories of Lenore;
Quaff, oh, quaff this kind nepenthe and forget this lost Lenore!"
      Quoth the Raven, "Nevermore."

"Prophet!" said I, "thing of evil!—prophet still, if bird or devil!—
Whether Tempter sent, or whether tempest tossed thee here ashore,
Desolate yet all undaunted, on this desert land enchanted—
On this home by Horror haunted—tell me truly, I implore—
Is there—*is* there balm in Gilead?—tell me—tell me, I implore!"
      Quoth the Raven, "Nevermore."

"Prophet!" said I, "thing of evil!—prophet still, if bird or devil!
By that Heaven that bends above us—by that God we both adore—
Tell this soul with sorrow laden if, within the distant Aidenn,
It shall clasp a sainted maiden whom the angels name Lenore—
Clasp a rare and radiant maiden whom the angels name Lenore."
      Quoth the Raven, "Nevermore."

"Be that word our sign of parting, bird or fiend!" I shrieked, upstarting—
"Get thee back into the tempest and the Night's Plutonian shore!
Leave no black plume as a token of that lie thy soul hath spoken!
Leave my loneliness unbroken!—quit the bust above my door!"
      Quoth the Raven, "Nevermore."

And the Raven, never flitting, still is sitting, *still* is sitting
On the pallid bust of Pallas just above my chamber door;
And his eyes have all the seeming of a demon's that is dreaming,
And the lamp-light o'er him streaming throws his shadow on the floor;
And my soul from out that shadow that lies floating on the floor
      Shall be lifted—nevermore!

—EDGAR ALLAN POE

Autumn

There is wind where the rose was;
Cold rain where sweet grass was;
    And clouds like sheep
    Stream o'er the steep
Grey skies where the lark was.

Nought gold where your hair was;
Nought warm where your hand was;
    But phantom, forlorn,
    Beneath the thorn,
Your ghost where your face was.

Sad winds where your voice was;
Tears, tears where my heart was;
    And ever with me,
    Child, ever with me,
Silence where hope was.

—WALTER DE LA MARE

Firefly

A little light is going by,
Is going up to see the sky,
A little light with wings.

I never could have thought of it,
To have a little bug all lit
And made to go on wings.

—ELIZABETH MADOX ROBERTS

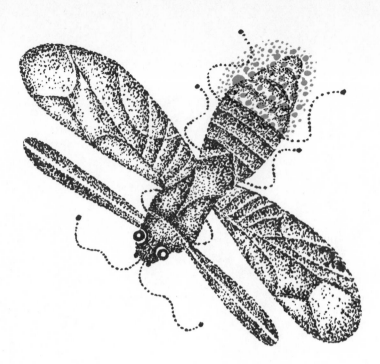

The Chair

A funny thing about a Chair:
You hardly ever think it's *there*.
To know a Chair is really it,
You sometimes have to go and sit.

—THEODORE ROETHKE

Oh, Fair to See

Oh, fair to see
Bloom-laden cherry tree,
    Arrayed in sunny white:
    An April day's delight,
Oh, fair to see!

Oh, fair to see
Fruit-laden cherry tree,
    With balls of shining red
    Decking a leafy head,
Oh, fair to see!

—CHRISTINA ROSSETTI

Sweet and Low

FROM *The Princess*

Sweet and low, sweet and low,
   Wind of the western sea,
Low, low, breathe and blow,
   Wind of the western sea!
Over the rolling waters go,
Come from the dying moon, and blow,
   Blow him again to me;
While my little one, while my pretty one, sleeps.

Sleep and rest, sleep and rest,
   Father will come to thee soon;
Rest, rest, on mother's breast,
   Father will come to thee soon;
Father will come to his babe in the nest,
Silver sails all out of the west
   Under the silver moon;
Sleep, my little one, sleep, my pretty one, sleep.

—ALFRED, LORD TENNYSON

Eletelephony

Once there was an elephant,
Who tried to use the telephant—
No! no! I mean an elephone
Who tried to use the telephone—
(Dear me! I am not certain quite
That **even** now I've got it right.)
Howe'**er** it was, he got his trunk
Entangled in the telephunk;
The more he tried to get it free,
The louder buzzed the telephee—
(I fear I'd better drop the song
Of elephop and telephong!)

—LAURA RICHARDS

Christmas Everywhere

Everywhere, everywhere, Christmas to-night!
Christmas in lands of the fir tree and pine,
Christmas in lands of the palm tree and vine,
Christmas where snow peaks stand solemn and white,
Christmas where cornfields lie sunny and bright!

Christmas where children are hopeful and gay,
Christmas where old men are patient and gray,
Christmas where peace, like a dove in his flight,
Broods o'er brave men in the thick of the fight,
Everywhere, everywhere, Christmas to-night.

For the Christ Child who comes is the Master of all;
No palace too great and no cottage too small.

— PHILLIPS BROOKS

Velvet Shoes

Let us walk in the white snow
In a soundless space;
With footsteps quiet and slow,
At a tranquil pace,
Under veils of white lace.

I shall go shod in silk,
And you in wool,
White as a white cow's milk,
More beautiful
Than the breast of a gull.

We shall walk through the still town
In a windless peace;
We shall step upon white down,
Upon silver fleece,
Upon softer than these.

We shall walk in velvet shoes:
Wherever we go
Silence will fall like dews
On white silence below.
We shall walk in the snow.

— ELINOR WYLIE

Jemima

There was a little girl who had a little curl,
Right in the middle of her forehead,
And when she was good, she was very, very good,
But when she was bad she was horrid.

One day she went upstairs, while her parents, unawares,
In the kitchen down below were at their meals,
And she stood upon her head, on her little truckle bed,
And she then began hurraying with her heels.

Her mother heard the noise, and thought it was the boys,
A-playing at a combat in the attic,
But when she climbed the stair and saw Jemima there,
She took and she did spank her most emphatic!

— HENRY WADSWORTH LONGFELLOW

Old Ironsides

WRITTEN IN PROTEST AGAINST THE PROPOSED
BREAKING UP OF THE FRIGATE CONSTITUTION.

Ay, tear her tattered ensign down!
Long has it waved on high,
And many an eye has danced to see
That banner in the sky;
Beneath it rung the battle shout,
And burst the cannon's roar;—
The meteor of the ocean air
Shall sweep the clouds no more.

Her deck, once red with heroes' blood,
Where knelt the vanquished foe,
When winds were hurrying o'er the flood,
And waves were white below,
No more shall feel the victor's tread,
Or know the conquered knee;—
The harpies of the shore shall pluck
The eagle of the sea!

Oh, better that her shattered hulk
Should sink beneath the wave;
Her thunders shook the mighty deep,
And there should be her grave;

Nail to the mast her holy flag,
Set every threadbare sail,
And give her to the god of storms,
The lightning and the gale!

—OLIVER WENDELL HOLMES

Epigram

Sir, I admit your general rule,
That every poet is a fool,
But you yourself may serve to show it,
That every fool is not a poet.

— ALEXANDER POPE

I Saw a Man Pursuing the Horizon

I saw a man pursuing the horizon;
Round and round they sped.
I was disturbed at this;
I accosted the man.
"It is futile," I said,
"You can never—"
"You lie," he cried,
And ran on.

— STEPHEN CRANE

The House on the Hill

They are all gone away,
    The House is shut and still,
There is nothing more to say.

Through broken walls and gray
    The winds blow bleak and shrill;
They are all gone away.

Nor is there anyone today
    To speak them good or ill:
There is nothing more to say.

Why is it then we stray
    Around that sunken sill?
They are all gone away,

And our poor fancy-play
    For them is wasted skill:
There is nothing more to say.

There is ruin and decay
    In the House on the Hill:
They are all gone away,
    There is nothing more to say.

—EDWIN ARLINGTON ROBINSON

I Hear America Singing

I hear America singing, the varied carols I hear,

Those of mechanics, each one singing his as it should be blithe and strong,

The carpenter singing his as he measures his plank or beam,

The mason singing his as he makes ready for work, or leaves off work,

The boatman singing what belongs to him in his boat, the deck-hand singing on the steamboat deck,

The shoemaker singing as he sits on his bench, the hatter singing as he stands,

The wood-cutter's song, the ploughboy's on his way in the morning, or at noon intermission or at sundown,

The delicious singing of the mother, or of the young wife at work, or of the girl sewing or washing,

Each singing what belongs to him or her and to none else,

The day what belongs to the day—at night the party of young fellows, robust, friendly,

Singing with open mouths their strong melodious songs.

—WALT WHITMAN

The Janitor's Boy

Oh I'm in love with the janitor's boy,
   And the janitor's boy loves me;
He's going to hunt for a desert isle
   In our geography.

A desert isle with spicy trees
   Somewhere near Sheepshead Bay;
A right nice place, just fit for two
   Where we can live alway.

Oh I'm in love with the janitor's boy,
   He's busy as he can be;
And down in the cellar he's making a raft
   Out of an old settee.

He'll carry me off, I know that he will,
   For his hair is exceedingly red;
And the only thing that occurs to me
   Is to dutifully shiver in bed.

The day that we sail, I shall leave this brief note,
   For my parents I hate to annoy:
"I have flown away to an isle in the bay
   With the janitor's red-haired boy."

— NATHALIA CRANE

Bed in Summer

In winter I get up at night.
And dress by yellow candle-light.
In summer, quite the other way,
I have to go to bed by day.

I have to go to bed and see
The birds still hopping on the tree.
Or hear the grown-up people's feet
Still going past me in the street.

And does it not seem hard to you,
When all the sky is clear and blue,
And I should like so much to play,
To have to go to bed by day?

—ROBERT LOUIS STEVENSON

The Last Word of a Bluebird

(As Told to a Child)

As I went out a Crow
In a low voice said "Oh,
I was looking for you.
How do you do?
I just came to tell you
To tell Lesley (will you?)
That her little Bluebird
Wanted me to bring word
That the north wind last night
That made the stars bright
And made ice on the trough

Almost made him cough
His tail feathers off.
He just had to fly!
But he sent her Good-bye,
And said to be good,
And wear her red hood,
And look for skunk tracks
In the snow with an axe—
And do everything!
And perhaps in the spring
He would come back and sing."

— ROBERT FROST

Molly Pitcher

'Twas hurry and scurry at Monmouth town,
  For Lee was beating a wild retreat;
The British were riding the Yankees down,
  And panic was pressing on flying feet.

Galloping down like a hurricane
  Washington rode with his sword swung high,
Mighty as he of the Trojan plain
  Fired by a courage from the sky.

"Halt, and stand to your guns!" he cried.
  And a bombardier made swift reply.
Wheeling his cannon into the tide,
  He fell 'neath the shot of a foeman nigh.

Molly Pitcher sprang to his side,
  Fired as she saw her husband do.
Telling the king in his stubborn pride
  Women like men to their homes are true.

Washington rode from the bloody fray
  Up to the gun that a woman manned.
"Molly Pitcher, you saved the day,"
  He said, as he gave her a hero's hand.

He named her sergeant with manly praise,
  While her war-brown face was wet with tears—
A woman has ever a woman's ways,
  And the army was wild with cheers.

—KATE BROWNLEE SHERWOOD

Written in March

The cock is crowing,
The stream is flowing,
The small birds twitter,
The lake doth glitter,
The green field sleeps in the sun;
The oldest and youngest
Are at work with the strongest;
The cattle are grazing,
Their heads never raising;
There are forty feeding like one!

Like an army defeated
The snow hath retreated,
And now doth fare ill
On the top of the bare hill;
The ploughboy is whooping — anon — anon;
There's joy in the mountains;
There's life in the fountains;
Small clouds are sailing,
Blue sky prevailing;
The rain is over and gone!

— WILLIAM WORDSWORTH

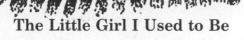

The Little Girl I Used to Be

The little girl I used to be
Had angels on her Christmas tree:

Ribbands of blue held her golden hair:
She was bounden round with silken care.

She finger-painted on frosty panes:
Thank-Thee'd for victuals in His Name,

And scraping her apple with a silver spoon
On never-ending afternoons,

Never knew, being only seven,
She was a resident of Heaven.

— MARGUERITE HARRIS

All in Green Went My Love Riding

All in green went my love riding
on a great horse of gold
into the silver dawn.

four lean hounds crouched low and smiling
the merry deer ran before.

Fleeter be they than dappled dreams
the swift sweet deer
the red rare deer.

Four red roebuck at a white water
the cruel bugle sang before.

Horn at hip went my love riding
riding the echo down
into the silver dawn.

four lean hounds crouched low and smiling
the level meadows ran before.

Softer be they than slippered sleep
the lean lithe deer
the fleet flown deer.

Four fleet does at a gold valley
the famished arrow sang before.

Bow at belt went my love riding
riding the mountain down
into the silver dawn.

four lean hounds crouched low and smiling
the sheer peaks ran before.

Paler be they than daunting death
the sleek slim deer
the tall tense deer.

Four tall stags at a green mountain
the lucky hunter sang before.

All in green went my love riding
on a great horse of gold
into the silver dawn.

four lean hounds crouched low and smiling
my heart fell dead before.

—E. E. CUMMINGS

At the Zoo

First I saw the white bear, then I saw the black;

Then I saw the camel with a hump upon his back;

Then I saw the grey wolf, with mutton in his maw;

Then I saw the wombat waddle in the straw;

Then I saw the elephant a-waving of his trunk;

Then I saw the monkeys—mercy, how unpleasantly they—smelt!

—WILLIAM MAKEPEACE THACKERAY

Robert, Who Is Often a Stranger to Himself

Do you ever look in the looking-glass
And see a stranger there?
A child you know and do not know,
Wearing what you wear?

—GWENDOLYN BROOKS

Where Go the Boats?

Dark brown is the river,
  Golden is the sand.
It flows along for ever,
  With trees on either hand.

Green leaves a-floating,
  Castles of the foam,
Boats of mine a-boating—
  Where will all come home?

On goes the river,
  And out past the mill,
Away down the valley,
  Away down the hill.

Away down the river,
  A hundred miles or more,
Other little children
  Shall bring my boats ashore.

—ROBERT LOUIS STEVENSON

Little Orphant Annie

Little Orphant Annie's come to our house to stay,
An' wash the cups an' saucers up, an' brush the crumbs away,
An' shoo the chickens off the porch, an' dust the hearth, an' sweep,
An' make the fire, an' bake the bread, an' earn her board-an'-keep;
An' all us other children, when the supper-things is done,
We set around the kitchen fire an' has the mostest fun
A-list'nin' to the witch-tales 'at Annie tells about,
An' the Gobble-uns 'at gits you
    Ef you
        Don't
            Watch
                Out!

Wunst they wuz a little boy wouldn't say his prayers,—
An' when he went to bed at night, away up-stairs,
His Mammy heered him holler, an' his Daddy heered him bawl,
An' when they turn't the kivvers down, he wuzn't there at all!
An' they seeked him in the rafter-room, an' cubby-hole, an' press,
An' seeked him up the chimbly-flue, an' ever'-wheres, I guess;
But all they ever found wuz thist his pants an' roundabout:—
An' the Gobble-uns 'll git you
    Ef you
        Don't
            Watch
                Out!

An' one time a little girl 'ud allus laugh an' grin,

An' make fun of ever' one, an' all her blood-an'-kin;

An' wunst, when they was "company," an' ole folks was there,

She mocked 'em an' shocked 'em, an' said she didn't care!

An' thist as she kicked her heels, an' turn't to run an' hide,

They was two great Black Things a-standin' by her side,

An' they snatched her through the ceilin' 'fore she knowed what she's about!

An' the Gobble-uns 'll git you

    Ef you

        Don't

            Watch

                Out!

An' little Orphant Annie says, when the blaze is blue,

An' the lamp-wick sputters, an' the wind goes *woo-oo!*

An' you hear the crickets quit, an' the moon is gray,

An' the lightnin'-bugs in dew is all squenched away,—

You better mind yer parunts, an' yer teachers fond an' dear,

An' churish them 'at loves you, an' dry the orphant's tear,

An' he'p the pore an' needy ones 'at clusters all about,

Er the Gobble-uns 'll git you

    Ef you

        Don't

            Watch

                Out!

—JAMES WHITCOMB RILEY

Growltiger's Last Stand

GROWLTIGER was a Bravo Cat, who lived upon a barge:
In fact he was the roughest cat that ever roamed at large.
From Gravesend up to Oxford he pursued his evil aims,
Rejoicing in his title of "The Terror of the Thames."

His manners and appearance did not calculate to please;
His coat was torn and seedy, he was baggy at the knees;
One ear was somewhat missing, no need to tell you why,
And he scowled upon a hostile world from one forbidding eye.

The cottagers of Rotherhithe knew something of his fame,
At Hammersmith and Putney people shuddered at his name.
They would fortify the hen-house, lock up the silly goose,
When the rumour ran along the shore: GROWLTIGER'S ON THE
   LOOSE!

Woe to the weak canary, that fluttered from its cage;
Woe to the pampered Pekinese, that faced Growltiger's rage.
Woe to the bristly Bandicoot, that lurks on foreign ships,
And woe to any Cat with whom Growltiger came to grips!

But most to Cats of foreign race his hatred had been vowed;
To Cats of foreign name and race no quarter was allowed.
The Persian and the Siamese regarded him with fear—
Because it was a Siamese had mauled his missing ear.

Now on a peaceful summer night, all nature seemed at play,
The tender moon was shining bright, the barge at Molesey lay.
All in the balmy moonlight it lay rocking on the tide—
And Growltiger was disposed to show his sentimental side.

His bucko mate, GRUMBUSKIN, long since had disappeared,
For to the Bell at Hampton he had gone to wet his beard;
And his bosun, TUMBLEBRUTUS, he too had stol'n away—
In the yard behind the Lion he was prowling for his prey.

In the forepeak of the vessel Growltiger sat alone,
Concentrating his attention on the Lady GRIDDLEBONE.
And his raffish crew were sleeping in their barrels and their bunks—
As the Siamese came creeping in their sampans and their junks.

Growltiger had no eye or ear for aught but Griddlebone,
And the Lady seemed enraptured by his manly baritone,
Disposed to relaxation, and awaiting no surprise—
But the moonlight shone reflected from a thousand bright blue eyes.

And closer still and closer the sampans circled round,
And yet from all the enemy there was not heard a sound.
The lovers sang their last duet, in danger of their lives—
For the foe was armed with toasting forks and cruel carving knives.

Then GILBERT gave the signal to his fierce Mongolian horde;
With a frightful burst of fireworks the Chinks they swarmed aboard.
Abandoning their sampans, and their pullaways and junks,
They battened down the hatches on the crew within their bunks.

Then Griddlebone she gave a screech, for she was badly skeered;
I am sorry to admit it, but she quickly disappeared.
She probably escaped with ease, I'm sure she was not drowned—
But a serried ring of flashing steel Growltiger did surround.

The ruthless foe pressed forward, in stubborn rank on rank;
Growltiger to his vast surprise was forced to walk the plank.
He who a hundred victims had driven to that drop,
At the end of all his crimes was forced to go ker-flip, ker-flop.

Oh there was joy in Wapping when the news flew through the land;
At Maidenhead and Henley there was dancing on the strand.
Rats were roasted whole at Brentford, and at Victoria Dock,
And a day of celebration was commanded in Bangkok.

—T.S. ELIOT

Da Boy from Rome

Today ees com' from Eetaly
    A boy ees leeve een Rome,
An' he ees stop an' speak weeth me—
    I weesh he stay at home.

He stop an' say "Hallo," to me,
    An' w'en he standin' dere
I smal da smal of Eetaly
    Steell steechin' een hees hair,
Dat com' weeth heem across da sea,
    An' een da clo'es he wear.

Da peopla bomp heem een da street,
    De noise ees scare heem, too;
He ees so clumsy een da feet
    He don't know w'at to do,
Dere ees so many theeng he meet
    Dat ees so strange, so new.

He sheever an' he ask eef here
    Eet ees so always cold.
Deen een hees eye ees com' a tear—
    He ees no vera old—
An', oh, hees voice ees soun' so queer
    I have no heart for scold.

He look up een da sky so gray,
    But oh, hees eye ees be
So far away, so far away,
    An' w'at he see I see.
Da sky eet ees no gray today
    At home een Eetaly.

He see da glada peopla seet
    Where warma shine da sky—
Oh, while he eesa look at eet
    He ees baygeen to cry.
Eef I no growl an' swear a beet
    So, too, my frand, would I.

Oh, why he stop an' speak weeth me,
    Dees boy dat leeve een Rome,
An' come today from Eetaly?
    I weesh he stay at home.

—THOMAS AUGUSTINE DALY

There Was a Naughty Boy

There was a naughty boy,
　A naughty boy was he,
He would not stop at home,
　He could not quiet be—
　　He took
　　In his knapsack
　　A book
　　Full of vowels
　　And a shirt
　　With some towels,
　　A slight cap
　　For night cap,
　　A hair brush,
　　Comb ditto,
　　New stockings—
　　For old ones
　　Would split O!
　　This knapsack
　　Tight at 's back
　　He rivetted close
And followed his nose
　To the North,
　To the North,
And followed his nose
　To the North.

Three Things to Remember

A Robin Redbreast in a cage
Puts all Heaven in a rage.

A skylark wounded on the wing
Doth make a cherub cease to sing.

He who shall hurt the little wren
Shall never be beloved by men.

— WILLIAM BLAKE

There was a naughty boy,
　　And a naughty boy was he,
He ran away to Scotland
　　The people for to see—
　　　There he found
　　　That the ground
　　　Was as hard,
　　　That a yard
　　　Was as long,
　　　That a song
　　　Was as merry,
　　　That a cherry
　　　Was as red—
　　　That lead
　　　Was as weighty
　　　That fourscore
　　　Was as eighty,
　　　That a door
　　　Was as wooden
　　　As in England—
So he stood in his shoes
　　And he wondered,
　　He wondered,
He stood in his shoes
　　And he wondered.

— JOHN KEATS

115

George Who Played with a Dangerous Toy,
and Suffered a Catastrophe of Considerable Dimensions

When George's Grandmamma was told
That George had been as good as Gold,
She Promised in the Afternoon
To buy him an *Immense* BALLOON.
And so she did; but when it came,
It got into the candle flame,
And being of a dangerous sort
Exploded with a Loud Report!
The Lights went out! The Windows broke!
The Room was filled with reeking smoke!
And in the darkness shrieks and yells
Were mingled with Electric Bells,
And falling masonry and groans,
And crunching, as of broken bones,
And dreadful shrieks, when, worst of all,
The House itself began to fall!
It tottered, shuddering to and fro,
Then crashed into the street below—
Which happened to be Savile Row.

When Help arrived, among the Dead
Were Cousin Mary, Little Fred,
The Footmen (both of them), the Groom,
The man that cleaned the Billiard-Room,
The Chaplain, and the Still-Room Maid.
And I am dreadfully afraid
That Monsieur Champignon, the Chef,
Will now be permanently deaf—
And both his Aides are much the same;
While George, who was in part to blame,
Received, you will regret to hear,
A nasty lump behind his ear.

The moral is that little Boys
Should not be given dangerous Toys.

—HILAIRE BELLOC

O Captain! My Captain!

O Captain! my Captain! our fearful trip is done,
The ship has weather'd every rack, the prize we sought is won,
The port is near, the bells I hear, the people all exulting,
While follow eyes the steady keel, the vessel grim and daring;
     But O heart! heart! heart!
       O the bleeding drops of red,
         Where on the deck my Captain lies,
           Fallen cold and dead.

O Captain! my Captain! rise up and hear the bells;
Rise up—for you the flag is flung—for you the bugle trills,
For you bouquets and ribbon'd wreaths—for you the shores a-crowding
For you they call, the swaying mass, their eager faces turning;
     Here Captain! dear father!
       The arm beneath your head!
         It is some dream that on the deck,
           You've fallen cold and dead.

My Captain does not answer, his lips are pale and still,
My father does not feel my arm, he has no pulse nor will,
The ship is anchor'd safe and sound, its voyage closed and done,
From fearful trip the victor ship comes in with object won:
     Exult O shores, and ring O bells!
       But I with mournful tread,
         Walk the deck my Captain lies,
           Fallen cold and dead.

—WALT WHITMAN

A Fence

Now the stone house on the lake front is finished and the workmen are beginning the
  fence.
The palings are made of iron bars with steel points that can stab the life out of any man
  that falls on them.
As a fence, it is a masterpiece, and will shut off the rabble and all vagabonds and
  hungry men and all wandering children looking for a place to play.
Passing through the bars and over the steel points will go nothing except Death and the
  Rain and To-morrow.

—CARL SANDBURG

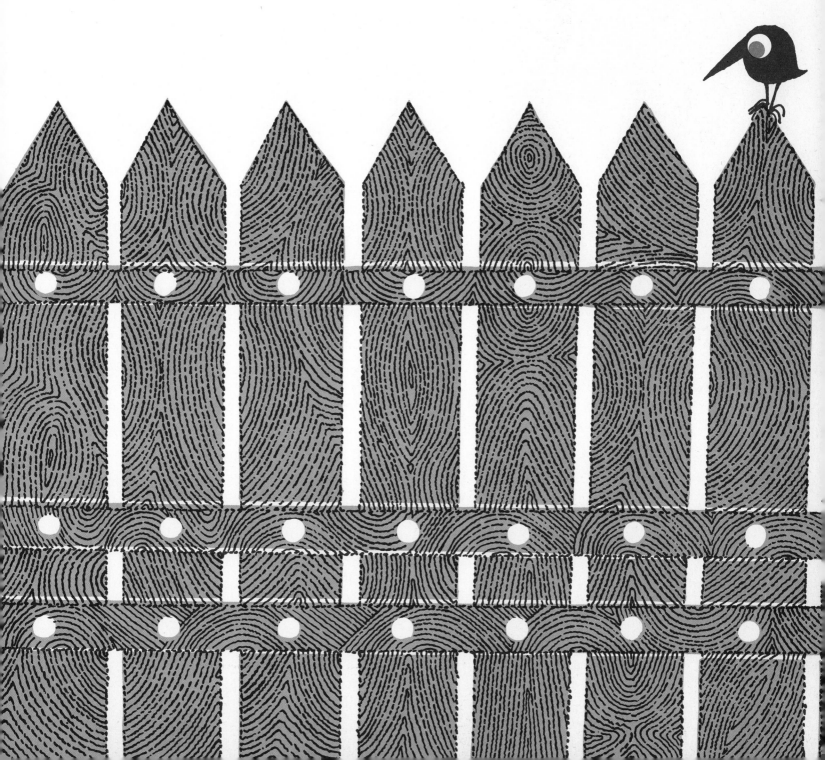

Paul Revere's Ride

Listen, my children, and you shall hear
Of the midnight ride of Paul Revere,
On the eighteenth of April, in Seventy-five;
Hardly a man is now alive
Who remembers that famous day and year.

He said to his friend, "If the British march
By land or sea from the town tonight,
Hang a lantern aloft in the belfry arch
Of the North Church tower as a signal light—
One, if by land, and two, if by sea;
And I on the opposite shore will be,
Ready to ride and spread the alarm
Through every Middlesex village and farm,
For the country folk to be up and to arm."

Then he said, "Good night!" and with muffled oar
Silently rowed to the Charlestown shore,
Just as the moon rose over the bay,
Where swinging wide at her moorings lay
The *Somerset*, British man-of-war;
A phantom ship, with each mast and spar
Across the moon like a prison bar,
And a huge black hulk, that was magnified
By its own reflection in the tide.

Hot Lunches
Jan. 3, 1989 to March 17, 1989

Hot Lunches will increase to $1.00 this fall. Bean burritos and cheese pizza will be offered during Lent.

Grade	name	T 1-6	P 1-13	Mc 1-20	H 1-27	T 2-3	P 2-10	B 2-24	P 3-3	B 3-10	P 3-17

SECOND

Taco   B = Bean Burrito
Pizza   H = Hot dog
Hamburger

Total Lunches _____
Total $ _____

Please return this form by Dec. 16, 1988
If you have any questions, please call Debbie Von Raesfeld, 247-9717

Meanwhile, his friend, through alley and street,
Wanders and watches, with eager ears,
Till in the silence around him he hears
The muster of men at the barrack door,
And the measured tread of the grenadiers,
Marching down to their boats on the shore.

Then he climbed to the tower of the Old North Church,
By the wooden stairs, with stealthy tread,
To the belfry-chamber overhead,
And startled the pigeons from their perch
On the somber rafters, that round him made
Masses and moving shapes of shade —
By the trembling ladder, steep and tall,
To the highest window in the wall,
Where he paused to listen and look down
A moment on the roofs of the town,
And the moonlight flowing over all.

Beneath in the churchyard, lay the dead,
In their night-encampment on the hill,
Wrapped in silence so deep and still
That he could hear, like a sentinel's tread,
The watchful night-wind, as it went
Creeping along from tent to tent,
And seeming to whisper, "All is well!"
A moment only he feels the spell
Of the place and the hour, and the secret dread
Of the lonely belfry and the dead;
For suddenly all his thoughts are bent
On a shadowy something far away,
Where the river widens to meet the bay —
A line of black that bends and floats
On the rising tide, like a bridge of boats.

Meanwhile, impatient to mount and ride,
Booted and spurred, with a heavy stride
On the opposite shore walked Paul Revere.
Now he patted his horse's side,
Now gazed at the landscape far and near,
Then, impetuous, stamped the earth,
And turned and tightened his saddle girth;
But mostly he watched with eager search
The belfry tower of the Old North Church,
As it rose above the graves on the hill,
Lonely and spectral and somber and still.

And lo! as he looks, on the belfry's height
A glimmer, and then a gleam of light!
He springs to the saddle, the bridle he turns,
But lingers and gazes, till full on his sight
A second lamp in the belfry burns!

A hurry of hoofs in a village street,
A shape in the moonlight, a bulk in the dark,
And beneath, from the pebbles, in passing, a spark
Struck out by a steed flying fearless and fleet:
That was all! And yet, through the gloom and the light,
The fate of a nation was riding that night;
And the spark struck out by that steed, in his flight,
Kindled the land into flame with its heat.

He has left the village and mounted the steep,
And beneath him, tranquil and broad and deep,
Is the Mystic, meeting the ocean tides;
And under the alders that skirt its edge,
Now soft on the sand, now loud on the ledge,
Is heard the tramp of his steed as he rides.

It was twelve by the village clock,
When he crossed the bridge into Medford town.
He heard the crowing of the cock,
And the barking of the farmer's dog,
And felt the damp of river fog,
That rises after the sun goes down.

It was one by the village clock,
When he galloped into Lexington.
He saw the gilded weathercock
Swim in the moonlight as he passed,
And the meeting-house windows, blank and bare,
Gaze at him with a spectral glare,
As if they already stood aghast
At the bloody work they would look upon.

It was two by the village clock,
When he came to the bridge in Concord town.
He heard the bleating of the flock,
And the twitter of birds among the trees,
And felt the breath of the morning breeze
Blowing over the meadows brown.
And one was safe and asleep in his bed
Who at the bridge would be first to fall,
Who that day would be lying dead,
Pierced by a British musket-ball.

You know the rest. In the books you have read
How the British Regulars fired and fled—
How the farmers gave them ball for ball,
From behind each fence and farmyard wall,
Chasing the red-coats down the lane,
Then crossing the fields to emerge again
Under the trees at the turn of the road,
And only pausing to fire and load.

So through the night rode Paul Revere;
And so through the night went his cry of alarm
To every Middlesex village and farm—
A cry of defiance and not of fear,
A voice in the darkness, a knock at the door,
And a word that shall echo for evermore!
For, borne on the night-wind of the Past,
Through all our history, to the last,
In the hour of darkness and peril and need,
The people will awaken and listen to hear
The hurrying hoof-beats of that steed,
And the midnight message of Paul Revere.

—HENRY WADSWORTH LONGFELLOW

Verse for a Certain Dog

Such glorious faith as fills your limpid eyes,
    Dear little friend of mine, I never knew.
All-innocent are you, and yet all-wise.
    (For Heaven's sake, stop worrying that shoe!)
You look about, and all you see is fair;
    This mighty globe was made for you alone.
Of all the thunderous ages, you're the heir.
    (Get off the pillow with that dirty bone!)

A skeptic world you face with steady gaze;
    High in young pride you hold your noble head,
Gayly you meet the rush of roaring days.
    (*Must* you eat puppy biscuit on the bed?)
Lancelike your courage, gleaming swift and strong.
    Yours the white rapture of a wingèd soul,
Yours is a spirit like a Mayday song.
    (God help you, if you break the goldfish bowl!)

"Whatever is, is good" — your gracious creed.
    You wear your joy of living like a crown.
Love lights your simplest act, your every deed.
    (Drop it, I tell you — put that kitten down!)
You are God's kindliest gift of all — a friend.
    Your shining loyalty unflecked by doubt,
You ask but leave to follow to the end.
    (Couldn't you wait until I took you out?)

— DOROTHY PARKER

124

The Bells

I

Hear the sledges with the bells—
    Silver Bells!
What a world of merriment their melody
    foretells!
    How they tinkle, tinkle, tinkle,
      In the icy air of night!
While the stars that oversprinkle
All the heavens, seem to twinkle
      With a crystalline delight;
      Keeping time, time, time,
      In a sort of Runic rhyme,
To the tintinnabulation that so musically
    wells
    From the bells, bells, bells, bells,
      Bells, bells, bells—
From the jingling and the tinkling of the
    bells.

II

Hear the mellow wedding bells—
    Golden bells!
What a world of happiness their harmony
    foretells!
    Through the balmy air of night
    How they ring out their delight!—
      From the molten-golden notes,
      And all in tune,
    What a liquid ditty floats
To the turtle-dove that listens, while she
    gloats
      On the moon!
Oh, from out the sounding cells,
What a gush of euphony voluminously
    wells!
    How it swells!

    How it dwells
    On the Future!—how it tells
    Of the rapture that impels
To the swinging and the ringing
    Of the bells, bells, bells,
Of the bells, bells, bells, bells,
    Bells, bells, bells—
To the rhyming and the chiming of the
    bells!

III

Hear the loud alarum bells—
    Brazen bells!
What a tale of terror, now their turbulency
    tells!
    In the startled ear of night
    How they scream out their affright!
      Too much horrified to speak,
      They can only shriek, shriek,
      Out of tune,
In a clamorous appealing to the mercy of
    the fire,
In a mad expostulation with the deaf and
    frantic fire,
      Leaping higher, higher, higher,
      With a desperate desire,
    And a resolute endeavor
Now—now to sit, or never,
By the side of the pale-faced moon.
    Oh, the bells, bells, bells!
    What a tale their terror tells
      Of Despair!
How they clang, and clash, and roar!
What a horror they outpour
On the bosom of the palpitating air!
    Yet the ear it fully knows,

By the twanging
And the clanging,
How the danger ebbs and flows;
Yet the ear distinctly tells,
In the jangling
And the wrangling,
How the danger sinks and swells,
By the sinking or the swelling in the anger
of the bells—
Of the bells—
Of the bells, bells, bells, bells,
Bells, bells, bells—
In the clamor and the clangor of the
bells!

IV

Hear the tolling of the bells—
Iron bells!
What a world of solemn thought their
monody compels!
In the silence of the night,
How we shiver with affright
At the melancholy menace of their
tone!
For every sound that floats
From the rust within their throats
Is a groan.
And the people—ah, the people—
They that dwell up in the steeple,
All alone,
And who tolling, tolling, tolling,
In that muffled monotone,
Feel a glory in so rolling
On the human heart a stone—
They are neither man nor woman—
They are neither brute nor human—

They are Ghouls:—
And their king it is who tolls:—
And he rolls, rolls, rolls,
Rolls
A pæan from the bells!
And his merry bosom swells
With the pæan of the bells!
And he dances, and he yells:
Keeping time, time, time,
In a sort of Runic rhyme,
To the pæan of the bells:—
Of the bells:
Keeping time, time, time
In a sort of Runic rhyme,
To the throbbing of the bells—
Of the bells, bells, bells—
To the sobbing of the bells:—
Keeping time, time, time,
As he knells, knells, knells,
In a happy Runic rhyme,
To the rolling of the bells—
Of the bells, bells, bells:—
To the tolling of the bells—
Of the bells, bells, bells, bells,
Bells, bells, bells—
To the moaning and the groaning of the
bells.

—EDGAR ALLAN POE

White Butterflies

Fly, white butterflies, out to sea,
Frail, pale wings for the wind to try,
Small white wings that we scarce can see,
       Fly!

Some fly light as a laugh of glee,
Some fly soft as a long, low sigh;
All to the haven where each would be,
       Fly!

— ALGERNON CHARLES SWINBURNE

There Is One that Has a Head
Without an Eye

There is one that has a head
   without an eye,
   And there's one that has an eye
   without a head:
You may find the answer if you try
   And when all is said,
   Half the answer hangs upon a thread.

—CHRISTINA ROSSETTI

The Snake

A narrow fellow in the grass
Occasionally rides;
You may have met him,—did you not,
His notice sudden is.

The grass divides as with a comb,
A spotted shaft is seen;
And then it closes at your feet
And opens further on.

He likes a boggy acre,
A floor too cool for corn.
Yet when a child, and barefoot,
I more than once, at morn,

Have passed, I thought, a whip-lash
Unbraiding in the sun,—
When, stooping to secure it,
It wrinkled, and was gone.

Several of nature's people
I know, and they know me;
I feel for them a transport
Of cordiality;

But never met this fellow,
Attended or alone,
Without a tighter breathing,
And zero at the bone.

—EMILY DICKINSON

Who Has Seen the Wind?

Who has seen the wind?
    Neither I nor you;
But when the leaves hang trembling
    The wind is passing thro'.

Who has seen the wind?
    Neither you nor I;
But when the trees bow down their heads
    The wind is passing by.

—CHRISTINA ROSSETTI

There Is a Garden in Her Face

There is a garden in her face
 Where roses and white lilies grow;
A heavenly paradise is that place
 Wherein all pleasant fruits do flow.
There cherries grow which none may buy,
Till "cherry-ripe" themselves do cry.

Those cherries fairly do enclose
 Of orient pearl a double row,
Which when her lovely laughter shows,
 They look like rosebuds filled with snow.
Yet them no peer nor prince can buy,
Till "cherry-ripe" themselves do cry.

Her eyes like angels watch them still,
 Her brows like bended bows do stand,
Threatening with piercing frowns to kill
 All that attempt, with eye or hand,
Those sacred cherries to come nigh,
Till "cherry-ripe" themselves do cry.

— THOMAS CAMPION

One Perfect Rose

A single flow'r he sent me, since we met.
　　All tenderly his messenger he chose;
Deep-hearted, pure, with scented dew still wet—
　　One perfect rose.

I knew the language of the floweret;
　　"My fragile leaves," it said, "his heart enclose."
Love long has taken for his amulet
　　One perfect rose.

Why is it no one ever sent me yet
　　One perfect limousine, do you suppose?
Ah no, it's always just my luck to get
　　One perfect rose.

—DOROTHY PARKER

Ariel's Dirge

Full fathom five thy father lies;
    Of his bones are coral made;
Those are pearls that were his eyes;
Nothing of him that doth fade
But doth suffer a sea-change
Into something rich and strange.
Sea-nymphs hourly ring his knell:
                Ding-dong.
Hark! now I hear them,—Ding-dong, bell.

— WILLIAM SHAKESPEARE

On His Books

When I am dead, I hope it may be said:
"His sins were scarlet, but his books were read."

— HILAIRE BELLOC

Cat & The Weather

Cat takes a look at the weather:
snow;

puts a paw on the sill;
his perch is piled, is a pillow.

Shape of his pad appears:
will it dig? No,

not like sand,

like his fur almost.

But licked, not liked:

too cold.

Insects are flying, fainting down.

He'll try

to bat one against the pane.

They have no body and no buzz,

and now his feet are wet;

it's a puzzle.

Shakes each leg,

then shakes his skin

to get the white flies off;

looks for his tail,

tells it to come on in

by the radiator.

World's turned queer

somehow: all white,

no smell. Well, here

inside it's still familiar.

He'll go to sleep until

it puts itself right.

—MAY SWENSON

The Ghosts of the Buffaloes

Last night at black midnight I woke with a cry,
The windows were shaking, there was thunder on high,
The floor was atremble, the door was ajar,
White fires, crimson fires, shone from afar.
I rushed to the dooryard. The city was gone.
My home was a hut without orchard or lawn.
It was mud-smear and logs near a whispering stream,
Nothing else built by man could I see in my dream . . .

Then . . .
Ghost-kings came headlong, row upon row,
Gods of the Indians, torches aglow.
They mounted the bear and the elk and the deer,
And eagles gigantic, aged and sere,
They rode long-horn cattle, they cried "A-la-la."
They lifted the knife, the bow, and the spear,
They lifted ghost-torches from dead fires below,
The midnight made grand with the cry "A-la-la."
The midnight made grand with a red-god charge,
A red-god show,
A red-god show,
"A-la-la, a-la-la, a-la-la, a-la-la."

With bodies like bronze, and terrible eyes
Came the rank and the file, with catamount cries,
Gibbering, yipping, with hollow-skull clacks,
Riding white bronchos with skeleton backs,

Scalp-hunters, beaded and spangled and bad,
Naked and lustful and foaming and mad,
Flashing primeval demoniac scorn,
Blood-thirst and pomp amid darkness reborn,
Power and glory that sleep in the grass
While the winds and the snows and the great rains pass.
They crossed the gray river, thousands abreast,
They rode out in infinite lines to the west,
Tide upon tide of strange fury and foam,
Spirits and wraiths, the blue was their home,
The sky was their goal where the star-flags are furled,
And on past those far golden splendors they whirled.
They burned to dim meteors, lost in the deep,
And I turned in dazed wonder, thinking of sleep.

And the wind crept by
Alone, unkempt, unsatisfied,
The wind cried and cried—
Muttered of massacres long past,
Buffaloes in shambles vast . . .
An owl said, "Hark, what is a-wing?"
I heard a cricket caroling,
I heard a cricket caroling,
I heard a cricket caroling.

Then . . .

Snuffing the lightning that crashed from on high

Rose royal old buffaloes, row upon row.

The lords of the prairie came galloping by.

And I cried in my heart "A-la-la, a-la-la.

A red-god show,

A red-god show,

A-la-la, a-la-la, a-la-la."

Buffaloes, buffaloes, thousands abreast,

A scourge and amazement, they swept to the west.

With black bobbing noses, with red rolling tongues,

Coughing forth steam from their leather-wrapped lungs,

Cows with their calves, bulls big and vain,

Goring the laggards, shaking the mane,

Stamping flint feet, flashing moon eyes,

Pompous and owlish, shaggy and wise.

Like sea-cliffs and caves resounded their ranks

With shoulders like waves, and undulant flanks.

Tide upon tide of strange fury and foam,

Spirits and wraiths, the blue was their home,

The sky was their goal where the star-flags are furled,

And on past those far golden splendors they whirled.

They burned to dim meteors, lost in the deep,

And I turned in dazed wonder, thinking of sleep.

I heard a cricket's cymbals play,

A scarecrow lightly flapped his rags,

And a pan that hung by his shoulder rang,

Rattled and thumped in a listless way,

And now the wind in the chimney sang,

The wind in the chimney,

The wind in the chimney,

The wind in the chimney,

Seemed to say:—

"Dream, boy, dream,

If you anywise can.

To dream is the work

Of beast or man.

Life is the west-going dream-storm's breath,

Life is a dream, the sigh of the skies,

The breath of the stars, that nod on their pillows

With their golden hair mussed over their eyes."

The locust played on his musical wing,

Sang to his mate of love's delight.

I heard the whippoorwill's soft fret.

I heard a cricket caroling,

I heard a cricket caroling,

I heard a cricket say: "Good-night, good-night,

Good-night, good-night, . . . good-night."

—VACHEL LINDSAY

There Was an Old Man of Dumbree

There was an Old Man of Dumbree,
Who taught little owls to drink tea;
    For he said, "To eat mice,
     Is not proper or nice,"
That amiable Man of Dumbree.

—EDWARD LEAR

Grizzly Bear

If you ever, ever, ever meet a grizzly bear,
You must never, never, never ask him *where*
He is going.
Or *what* he is doing;
For if you ever, ever dare
To stop a grizzly bear,
You will never meet *another* grizzly bear.

— MARY AUSTIN

Mr. Macklin's Jack O'Lantern

Mr. Macklin takes his knife
And carves the yellow pumpkin face:
Three holes bring eyes and nose to life,
The mouth has thirteen teeth in place.

Then Mr. Macklin just for fun
Transfers the corn-cob pipe from his
Wry mouth to Jack's, and everyone
Dies laughing! O what fun it is

Till Mr. Macklin draws the shade
And lights the candle in Jack's skull.
Then all the inside dark is made
As spooky and as horrorful

As Halloween, and creepy crawl
The shadows on the tool-house floor,
With Jack's face dancing on the wall.
O Mr. Macklin! where's the door?

—DAVID MCCORD

There Was an Old Man in a Tree

There was an Old Man in a tree,
Who was horribly bored by a bee;
    When they said, "Does it buzz?"
    He replied, "Yes, it does!
It's a regular brute of a bee!"

—EDWARD LEAR

Casey at the Bat

The outlook wasn't brilliant for the Mudville nine that day;
The score stood four to two with but one inning more to play.
And then when Cooney died at first and Barrows did the same,
A sickly silence fell upon the patrons of the game.

A straggling few got up to go in deep despair. The rest
Clung to the hope which springs eternal in the human breast;
They thought if only Casey could but get a whack at that—
We'd put up even money now with Casey at the bat.

But Flynn preceded Casey, as did also Jimmy Blake,
And the former was a lulu and the latter was a cake;
So upon that stricken multitude grim melancholy sat,
For there seemed but little chance of Casey's getting to the bat.

But Flynn let drive a single, to the wonderment of all,
And Blake, the much despisèd, tore the cover off the ball;
And when the dust had lifted, and the men saw what had occurred,
There was Jimmy safe at second and Flynn a-hugging third.

145

Then from five thousand throats and more there rose a lusty yell;
It rumbled through the valley, it rattled in the dell;
It knocked upon the mountain and recoiled upon the flat,
For Casey, mighty Casey, was advancing to the bat.

There was ease in Casey's manner as he stepped into his place;
There was pride in Casey's bearing and a smile on Casey's face.
And when, responding to the cheers, he lightly doffed his hat,
No stranger in the crowd could doubt 'twas Casey at the bat.

Ten thousand eyes were on him as he rubbed his hands with dirt;
Five thousand tongues applauded when he wiped them on his shirt.
Then while the writhing pitcher ground the ball into his hip,
Defiance gleamed in Casey's eye, a sneer curled Casey's lip.

And now the leather-covered sphere came hurtling through the air,
And Casey stood a-watching it in haughty grandeur there.
Close by the sturdy batsman the ball unheeded sped—
"That ain't my style," said Casey. "Strike one," the umpire said.

From the benches, black with people, there went up a muffled roar,
Like the beating of the storm waves on a stern and distant shore.

"Kill him! Kill the umpire!" shouted someone on the stand;
And it's likely they'd have killed him had not Casey raised his hand.

With a smile of Christian charity great Casey's visage shone;
He stilled the rising tumult; he bade the game go on;
He signaled to the pitcher, and once more the spheroid flew;
But Casey still ignored it, and the umpire said, "Strike two."

"Fraud!" cried the maddened thousands, and echo answered, "Fraud!"
But one scornful look from Casey and the audience was awed.
They saw his face grow stern and cold, they saw his muscles strain,
And they knew that Casey wouldn't let that ball go by again.

The sneer is gone from Casey's lip, his teeth are clenched in hate;
He pounds with cruel violence his bat upon the plate.
And now the pitcher holds the ball, and now he lets it go,
And now the air is shattered by the force of Casey's blow.

Oh, somewhere in this favored land the sun is shining bright;
The band is playing somewhere, and somewhere hearts are light,
And somewhere men are laughing, and somewhere children shout;
But there is no joy in Mudville—mighty Casey has struck out.

—ERNEST LAWRENCE THAYER

Acknowledgments

Rand McNally, publisher of ILLUSTRATED POEMS FOR CHILDREN, wishes to thank the following authors, publishers, and agents for permission to reprint copyrighted material. Every possible effort has been made to trace the ownership of each poem included. If any errors or omissions have occurred, correction will be made in subsequent editions, provided that the publisher is notified of their existence.

The Belknap Press of Harvard University Press for "I'm nobody! Who are you?" from *The Poems of Emily Dickinson*, edited by Thomas H. Johnson; reprinted by permission of the publishers and the Trustees of Amherst College, copyright 1951 and 1955 by the President and Fellows of Harvard College.

The Bobbs-Merrill Company, Inc., for "The Raggedy Man" and "Little Orphant Annie" from *Joyful Poems for Children* by James Whitcomb Riley, copyright 1941, 1946, and 1960 by Lesley Payne, Elizabeth Eitel Miesse, and Edmund H. Eitel.

Doubleday & Company, Inc., for "I Hear America Singing" and "O Captain! My Captain!" from *Leaves of Grass* by Walt Whitman, copyright 1924 by Doubleday & Company, Inc.

Doubleday & Company, Inc., and Faber & Faber Ltd., London, for "The Bat" from *The Waking: Poems 1933-1953* by Theodore Roethke, copyright 1938, 1939, and 1953 by Theodore Roethke; and for "The Chair" by Theodore Roethke, copyright 1950 by Theodore Roethke.

Norma Millay Ellis for "Look, Edwin!" from *Collected Poems* by Edna St. Vincent Millay, published by Harper & Row, copyright 1929, 1956, by Edna St. Vincent Millay and Norma Millay Ellis.

Robert Graves for "The Six Badgers" from *The Penny Fiddle* by Robert Graves.

Harcourt Brace Jovanovich, Inc., for "Da Boy from Rome" from *Selected Poems of T. A. Daly*, copyright 1936 by Harcourt Brace Jovanovich, Inc., renewed 1964 by Thomas A. Daly, Jr.; and for "The Fence" from *Chicago Poems* by Carl Sandburg, copyright 1916 by Holt, Rinehart and Winston, Inc., renewed 1944 by Carl Sandburg.

Harcourt Brace Jovanovich, Inc., and Faber & Faber Ltd., London, for "In Just-" and "all in green went my love riding" from *Complete Poems 1913-1962* by E. E. Cummings, copyright 1923, 1951 by E. E. Cummings.

Harcourt Brace Jovanovich, Inc., and MacGibbon and Kee Ltd., London, for "Growltiger's Last Stand" from *Old Possum's Book of Practical Cats* by T. S. Eliot, copyright 1939 by T. S. Eliot, copyright 1967 by Esme Valerie Eliot.

Harper & Row, Publishers, Inc., for "Rudolph Is Tired of the City" and "Robert, Who Is Often a Stranger to Himself" from *Bronzeville Boys and Girls* by Gwendolyn Brooks, copyright 1956 by Gwendolyn Brooks Blakely.

Holt, Rinehart and Winston, Inc., and Jonathan Cape Ltd., London, for "Stopping by Woods on a Snowy Evening" and "The Last Word of a Bluebird" from *The Poetry of Robert Frost*, edited by Edward Connery Lathem, copyright 1916, 1923, and 1969 by Holt, Rinehart and Winston, Inc., copyright 1944 and 1951 by Robert Frost.

Holt, Rinehart and Winston, Inc., The Society of Authors, London, as literary representatives of the estate of A. E. Housman, and Jonathan Cape Ltd., London, for "The Street Sounds to the Soldiers' Tread" from *A Shropshire Lad* by A. E. Housman, copyright 1939, 1940, and 1959 by Holt, Rinehart and Winston, Inc., copyright 1967 by Robert E. Symons.

Houghton Mifflin Company for "The Grizzly Bear" from *The Children Sing in the Far West* by Mary Austin, copyright 1928 by Mary Austin, renewed 1956 by Kenneth M. Chapman.

Hubbard Press for "Snow" from *Be Nice to Spiders, Be Kind to Snakes and 26 Other Songs* by Stephen Titra, copyright 1973 by Hubbard Press.

Alfred A. Knopf, Inc., for "Spanish Johnny" from *April Twilights* by Willa Cather, copyright 1923 by Willa Cather, renewed 1951 by the executors of the estate of Willa Cather; and for "Velvet Shoes" from *Collected Poems of Elinor Wylie*, copyright 1921 and 1932 by Alfred A. Knopf, Inc.

Poems About . . .

151

(APPENDIX B)

Poems That Are...

Exciting

Frightening

Funny

Index <small>(TITLES)</small>

157

Index (FIRST LINES)